Diet recommendations during kidney cancer

Diet can support the affected organs and is not a treatment for the disease.
Please check these recommendations always with a nutrition consultant, therapist, doctor or dietician. The recipes and the list of ingredients are supporting the conventional medical therapy.
The calorie disclosures of fresh ingredients (fruit and vegetables) vary according to quality and time of harvest. The contents were checked by a dietician and a nutrition consultant for the Traditional Chinese Medicine (TCM).

Author:
©2019 Josef Miligui
www.ebns.at

AF220864

Source:
The lists are created from the EBNS database for nutritional counseling. The database is used by dietitians, therapists and doctors for advising the patient / client.

Literature:
The specialist literature and the training documents of the German and Austrian dietary and traditional Chinese medicine serve as a knowledge base. We have used the documents as a basis of knowledge, adapted it to our experience and completed them.
http://di-book.com

Production and publishing:
BoD – Books on Demand, Norderstedt
ISBN: 9783752861587

Diet recommendations during kidney cancer

1 Treatment strategy

Protein-standardized diet (0.8 g per kg) with special consideration of biological value and adequate energy intake; sodium, phosphate and low potassium drinks and foods. Immune-strengthening, infection-inhibiting diet.

2 Avoid

Sodium, potassium and phosphorus-rich foods and drinks. Organic low quality protein.

3 Breakfast

	kkal. per serving
Apricot and cranberry ice cream	106
Avocado with lemon	289
Baked chicory	230
Boiled celery salad with exotic spices	165
Carrot and potato rucola sandwich	94
Carrot and rice gruel soup	101
Carrot drink	143
Carrot Risotto	308
Champignon rice	410

4   Snack

5   Lunch

6   Afternoon

7   Dinner

8 Any time

9 Recipes

(rec.) = You can use more.
(little) = You should use less than specified
(no) omit.

9.1 Antipasti

Improves blood circulation, anti-inflammatory, relieves pain. Diuretic,
promotes digestion, reduces blood pressure, antioxidative, antibacterial,
affects anorexia, improves digestion, flatulence, stomach weakness,
stimulating.
Cooking time approx. 40 min
3 portions to 246,67g. / 100kcal. - (carb:54% / prot:46%)
100g.=40,54kcal. / protein 2,74g. fat:5,6g.
µg. - Ph:7,93 Na:1,08 Ka:67,54 Mg:5,14 Ca:7,21 Fe:0,24 Zn:0,03 Col.:0 Hsr.:5,8

Quantity of ingredients:
Pepperoni 1 piece / 5g. (yes)
Lemon juice 1 table spoon / 10g. (yes)
Aubergine 1 piece / 300g. (yes)
Tomato 4 pieces / 200g. (yes)
Zucchini 5/8 oz / 200g. (yes)
Lemon peel 1/2 piece / 3g. (yes)
Olive oil 1 table spoon / 15g. (yes)
Basil (fresh) 8 leaves / 5g. (yes)
Salt 1 pinch / 0,5g. (little)
Coriander 1/2 teaspoon / 2g. (yes)

Cooking instructions:
Preheat the oven to 250 degrees Celsius and bake the hot peppers until
the bowl becomes dark (about 20 minutes). Cover the hot peppers with
a clear film and allow to cool. Peel the skin and cut into strips about 2
cm wide. Cut tomatoes in half and spread with oil in slices of aubergine
and bake in the oven at 200 degrees golden brown (about 10 minutes)
Fry the zucchini slices in the grill pan (without fat).
Mix everything together, mix the marinade of olive oil, salt and lemon
peel and pour over the vegetables, sprinkle with coriander. Leave for 1
hour.

9.2 Apricot and cranberry ice cream

Forces resistance to infections, good to fight oral mucosal inflammation, diarrhea. Has a positive effect on the urinary tract.
Cooking time approx. 5 min
2 portions to 222,5g. / 106kcal. - (carb:91% / prot:9%)
100g.=47,87kcal. / protein 1,9g. fat:0,48g.
µg. - Ph:7,98 Na:0,94 Ka:107,17 Mg:4,69 Ca:8,02 Fe:0,03 Zn:0 Col.:0 Hsr.:8,57

Quantity of ingredients:
Apricots 3/4 lbs / 350g. (little)
Water 1/4 cup / 50g. (yes)
Cranberry 3 table spoons / 45g. (little)

Cooking instructions:
Mix the apricot juice with the cranberry syrup. Fill the juice into little molds, place in the freezer and let it freeze in about 3 hours.

9.3 Asparagus Cream Soup

Diuretic, improves blood circulation, prevents cancer, laxative, antiparasitic, stimulates liver function, good to fight loss of appetite, flatulence, rheumatism, heartburn.
Cooking time approx. 45 min
Allergens: ACG
2 portions to 409,5g. / 240kcal. - (carb:21% / prot:79%)
100g.=58,61kcal. / protein 5,2g. fat:19,85g.
µg. - Ph:9,44 Na:1,5 Ka:15,8 Mg:1,6 Ca:6,23 Fe:0,13 Zn:0,08 Col.:9,84 Hsr.:2,42

Quantity of ingredients:
Asparagus (green or white) 5/8 oz / 200g. (yes)
Water 2 cup / 500g. (yes)
Rapeseed oil 3 table spoons / 30g. (yes)
Wheat flour 2 table spoons / 10g. (yes)
Chicken yolk 1 piece / 25g. (yes)
Cow's milk (whole milk 3.5% fat) 1 table spoon / 15g. (little)
Sour cream 15% fat 1 table spoon / 15g. (little)
Pepper (ground) 1 pinch / 0,5g. ()
Nutmeg 1 pinch / 0,5g. (yes)
Lemon juice 1 teaspoon / 2g. (yes)
Parsley 2 table spoons / 20g. (yes)
Salt 1 pinch / 1g. (little)

Cooking instructions:
Wash and peel the asparagus.
Heat water, a little lemon juice and pinch of salt till it boils. Tie the asparagus spears together.
Add the asparagus peel to the cooking water and bring to the boil.
Add the asparagus and cook on low heat for about 20 minutes.
Then remove the asparagus bunches and pour the broth through a sieve.
For the roux, heat the oil in a saucepan, add the flour and sauté until it is colorless, slowly top up with the asparagus sauce and simmer for 10 minutes. Cut the asparagus spears into pieces about 3 cm long and place them to the soup.

Just before serving, bring the soup to the boil again.
Mix the egg yolk with the milk and sour cream.
Remove the pot from the heat and stir in the egg yolk and milk mixture.
Season with pepper and nutmeg, decorate with the chopped parsley and serve immediately.

9.4   Avocado with lemon

Good to fight insomnia, inflammation, swelling, pain and itching. Is calming.
Cooking time approx. 5 min
1 portion to 131g. / 289kcal. - (carb:17% / prot:83%)
100g.=220,61kcal. / protein 2,34g. fat:28,24g.
µg. - Ph:37,02 Na:5,86 Ka:469,27 Mg:29,31 Ca:11,83 Fe:0,59 Zn:0,37 Col.:0 Hsr.:29,01

Quantity of ingredients:
Avocado 1/2 piece / 120g. (yes)
Lemon juice 1/2 piece / 10g. (yes)
Salt 1 pinch / 1g. (little)

Cooking instructions:
Halve the avocado, remove the core, add the lemon juice, salt a little and eat with a spoon.

9.5 Baked chicory

Mineral supporter and is full of A-B-C vitamins.
Cooking time approx. 20 min
Allergens: AG
2 portions to 460,5g. / 230kcal. - (carb:74% / prot:26%)
100g.=50,05kcal. / protein 6,05g. fat:7,04g.
µg. - Ph:10,03 Na:4,19 Ka:30,57 Mg:4,66 Ca:5,41 Fe:0,15 Zn:0,07 Col.:0 Hsr.:4,48

Quantity of ingredients:
Chicory 4 pieces / 500g. (yes)
Cream, sweet 30% 2 table spoons / 40g. (little)
Breadcrumbs (wheat bread, bread roll) 2 table spoons / 20g. (yes)
Rice Basmati 1/2 cup / 60g. (yes)
Water 3 cups / 300g. (yes)
Salt 1 pinch / 1g. (little)

Cooking instructions:
Blanch chicory in hot water whole for about 5 minutes; place in a
casserole dish; put some sweet cream over it; put the bread crumbs
over the chicory and gratinate.

Place the rice in salted water, heat till it boils and let it simmer over low
heat for about 15 minutes.

9.6 Basic recipe for a reissue soup (Congee)

Low fat content, for the drainage of the body overweight and high blood
pressure.
Cooking time approx. 2-4 hours
3 portions to 273,33g. / 140kcal. - (carb:90% / prot:10%)
100g.=51,34kcal. / protein 2,96g. fat:0,48g.
µg. - Ph:1,95 Na:0,19 Ka:1,67 Mg:1,14 Ca:0,57 Fe:0,01 Zn:0,02 Col.:0 Hsr.:2,11

Quantity of ingredients:
Rice variety any 1 cup / 120g. (yes)
Water 6 cups / 700g. (yes)

Cooking instructions:
Cook rice and water in a ratio of about 1: 6. The amount of water
determines the thickness of the mash (matter of taste).
Put the rice in a saucepan with a heavy lid. It is important to simmer the
rice after a short boil on the slightest flame, otherwise it burns.
Boil the rice for 2-4 hours. The longer it cooks, the more it strengthens.
If you want to eat the dish for breakfast, you can put the rice on just

before bedtime.
To be on the safe side, you should first check the behavior of your pot and cooker under observation for a similar amount of time, so that nothing burns. Refrigerate for later use.

9.7 Basic recipe for a vegetable soup, nutritious

Reduces blood pressure, strengthens immune system, prevents cancer, forcing spleen, dissolves stagnation, promotes weight loss. Good to fight immunodeficiency, high blood pressure, depressions, diabetes, diarrhea, reduces blood lipids.
Cooking time approx. 2-3 hours
Allergens: L
5 portions to 240,6g. / 48kcal. - (carb:71% / prot:29%)
100g.=19,87kcal. / protein 1,56g. fat:1,31g.
µg. - Ph:0,97 Na:0,73 Ka:5,14 Mg:0,36 Ca:1,26 Fe:0,02 Zn:0,01 Col.:0 Hsr.:0,56

Quantity of ingredients:
Olive oil 1 table spoon / 4g. (yes)
Onion white 1 piece / 60g. (yes)
Carrot 3 pieces / 200g. (yes)
Parsnip 3/8 lbs - 6oz / 150g. (yes)
Celery root 1 cup / 100g. (yes)
Ginger fresh 1/2 teaspoon / 2g. (yes)
Lemon 1/2 piece / 25g. (yes)
Juniper berry 6 pieces / 6g. (yes)
Thyme dried 1 pinch / 1g. (yes)
Lovage 1 table spoon / 3g. (yes)
Bay leaf 2 leaves / 1g. (yes)
Salt 1 pinch / 1g. (little)
Water 3 cups / 650g. (yes)

Cooking instructions:
Cut the vegetables into cubes.
Heat oil in hot pot, fry shortly onions and vegetables.
Add cold water, then add ginger, bay leaf and lemon juice.
Season with juniper, thyme and lovage. Cover for 2 - 3 hours on a low heat and simmer.
The used vegetables should be thrown away.
The basic recipe serves as a soup base and to refine vegetables, legumes or cereals.
If you want to eat vegetable soup immediately, add the desired vegetables half an hour before.
Refrigerate for later use.

9.8   Basmati rice + Zucchini tofu dish

Diuretic, supports urination, harmonizes spleen and stomach, reduces flatulence, good to fight body overweight and high blood pressure. Antioxidative, promotes digestion, perspiration, reduces blood lipids, forcing spleen.
Cooking time approx. 20 min
Allergens: E
4 portions to 306,75g. / 146kcal. - (carb:57% / prot:43%)
100g.=47,51kcal. / protein 7,95g. fat:4,89g.
µg. - Ph:13,21 Na:0,7 Ka:33,77 Mg:10,99 Ca:11,98 Fe:0,34 Zn:0,02 Col.:0 Hsr.:7,75

Quantity of ingredients:
Soy Tofu 5/8 lbs - 8oz / 250g. (little)
Olive oil 2 table spoons / 6g. (yes)
Coriander 1/2 teaspoon / 4g. (yes)
Ginger fresh 1/2 teaspoon / 4g. (yes)
Rice Basmati 1/2 cup / 60g. (yes)
Water 3 cups / 200g. (yes)
Zucchini 1 piece / 700g. (yes)

Cooking instructions:
Cut tofu cubes and marinate with olive oil, tamari, crushed coriander and ginger. Leave at least 1 hour.

Cook Basmati rice with the water. You can season with onion and cardamom.
Roast zucchini and tofu in pan in the hot oil for approx. 5-7 min.
Serve rice and tofu on a plate.
Add the parsley.

Can also be used as a salad for the home and on the go.

9.9   Bitter lemon drink

Appetizing
Cooking time approx. 5 min
1 portion to 250g. / 130kcal. - (carb:93% / prot:7%)
100g.=52kcal. / protein 2,5g. fat:0g.
µg. - Ph:6 Na:4 Ka:1 Mg:1 Ca:4 Fe:0 Zn:0 Col.:0 Hsr.:0

Quantity of ingredients:
Bitter Lemon 1 cup / 250g. (yes)

9.10 Bitter melon with tomato vegetables

Against diabetes in old age, constipation, infections. Promotes digestion, stimulates, warms, antispasmodic, appetizing.
Cooking time approx. 30 min.
Allergens: G
2 portions to 274,5g. / 176kcal. - (carb:47% / prot:53%)
100g.=64,3kcal. / protein 3,69g. fat:12,18g.
µg. - Ph:10,36 Na:3,24 Ka:55,42 Mg:5,01 Ca:10,32 Fe:0,17 Zn:0,05 Col.:0,26 Hsr.:1,9

Quantity of ingredients:
Bitter melon 2 pieces / 250g. (rec.)
Tomato 2 pieces / 200g. (yes)
Yogurt (natural, 3.5% fat) 4 table spoons / 40g. (yes)
Corn germ oil 3 table spoons / 20g. (yes)
Lemon 1 piece / 5g. (yes)
Garlic 4 pieces / 5g. (yes)
Ginger fresh 1/2 oz / 10g. (yes)
Chili (pod or ground) 1/2 teaspoon / 2g. (yes)
Coriander 1 table spoon / 5g. (yes)
Cardamom 1 table spoon / 5g. (little)
Cumin (Caraway seed) 1 table spoon / 5g. (yes)
Saffron 1g. Or 0,034oz / 1g. (little)
Salt 1 pinch / 1g. (little)
Pepper (ground) 1 pinch / 0,5g. ()

Cooking instructions:
Cut the bitter melon in halfs, core it and cut it into strips. Then cut into small cubes. Cut the tomatoes into small pieces. Cut the chili into thin rings. Finely chop the garlic. Peel and finely slice the ginger.
In a saucepan with the oil, stir in the bitter cucumbers. Add tomatoes, garlic, ginger and salt. Simmer for 15 minutes. Stir in the spices and the lemon juice.

This fits rice or potatoes.

9.11 Boiled celery salad with exotic spices

Forcing spleen, relieves diarrhea, antibacterial, blood-forming, blood detoxifying, reduces inflammation, diuretic, improves blood circulation.
Cooking time approx. 30 min
Allergens: GLMNO
4 portions to 341g. / 166kcal. - (carb:48% / prot:52%)
100g.=48,61kcal. / protein 5,59g. fat:9,17g.
µg. - Ph:3,39 Na:6,17 Ka:17,47 Mg:0,76 Ca:5,05 Fe:0,03 Zn:0,01 Col.:0,2 Hsr.:3,02

Quantity of ingredients:
Celery root 1 1/2 piece / 900g. (yes)
Yogurt (natural, 3.5% fat) 1 cup / 250g. (yes)
Sour cream 15% fat 2 table spoons / 20g. (little)
Turmeric (yellow root) 1 pinch / 1g. (little)
Sesame oil 1 table spoon / 20g. (little)
Pepper (ground) 1 pinch / 0,5g. ()
Lemongrass 1 pinch / 1g. (yes)
Onion white 1/2 piece / 25g. (yes)
Mustard 1/2 teaspoon / 1g. (little)
Black caraway 1 pinch / 1g. (yes)
Salt 1 pinch / 1g. (little)
Lemon juice 1 piece / 40g. (yes)
Apple (sour) 1/2 piece / 100g. (little)
Peppers powder 1 pinch / 1g. (little)
Vinegar (Apple vinegar) 1 dash / 3g. (yes)

Cooking instructions:
Cook the peeled celeriac in thick slices and then cut into bite-sized strips.

Dressing: Mix a little yoghurt, sour cream, turmeric, sesame oil, pepper, lemongrass powder, finely chopped onion, a little mustard, salt, crushed black cumin, some cold water, lemon juice or vinegar; add the sour chopped apple, some rose paprika, the lukewarm celery and mix well; let it rest for 2 - 3 hours or overnight.

Ideal as a substitute for raw food

9.12 Carrot and potato rucola sandwich

Reduces inflammation, improves digestion, supports urination, lowers cholesterol, strengthens immune system, prevents cancer, good to fight constipation (Fibre-rich), dissolves stagnation.
Cooking time approx. 20 min
Allergens: AG
4 portions to 116,25g. / 94kcal. - (carb:55% / prot:45%)
100g.=80,86kcal. / protein 2,68g. fat:2,83g.
µg. - Ph:4,15 Na:4,56 Ka:16,7 Mg:1,23 Ca:1,78 Fe:0,06 Zn:0,03 Col.:0,25 Hsr.:1,27

Quantity of ingredients:
Potato (mealy) 5/8 oz / 200g. (little)
Carrot 1 piece / 50g. (yes)
Sour cream 15% fat 3 table spoons / 45g. (little)
Onion (spring onion) 1 piece / 20g. (yes)
Rucola 1/2 bunch / 100g. ()
Lemon peel 1/4 teaspoon / 1g. (yes)
Salt 1 pinch / 1g. (little)
Pepper (ground) 1 pinch / 0,2g. ()
Whole grain bread 8 slices / 48g. (little)

Cooking instructions:
Cook the potatoes gently, peel and squeeze through the potato press.
Cook vegetable broth according to the basic recipe and remove a carrot after a short cooking time and finely crush with a fork.
Stir the potatoes, carrots, grated lemon zest and sour cream into a smooth cream.
Mix carrot and potato cream with finely chopped rocket salad. Season the spread with salt and pepper and spread the bread. Sprinkle with the finely chopped young onions.

9.13 Carrot and rice gruel soup

Stops diarrhea, good to fight fever, strengthens immune system, reduces blood pressure.
Cooking time approx. 10 min
1 portion to 224g. / 101kcal. - (carb:96% / prot:4%)
100g.=45,09kcal. / protein 2,37g. fat:0,4g.
µg. - Ph:27,48 Na:20,34 Ka:65,63 Mg:170,89 Ca:178,57 Fe:1,03 Zn:0,34 Col.:0 Hsr.:12,3

Quantity of ingredients:
Basic recipe for a rice soup (Congee) 1 cup / 120g. (little)
Carrot 2 pieces / 100g. (yes)
Salt 1 teaspoon / 4g. (little)

Cooking instructions:
Peel and grate carrots. Heat the rice soup (according to the basic recipe) till it boils and add the grated carrots and salt. Cook for 10 minutes.

9.14 Carrot drink

Promotes spleen and liver, reduces blood pressure, strengthens immune system, prevents cancer, reduces radiation damage, diuretic, building up, eye-enhancing, detoxifying, nerve-strengthening.
Cooking time approx. 15 min
Allergens: H
1 portion to 265g. / 143kcal. - (carb:81% / prot:19%)
100g.=53,96kcal. / protein 3,78g. fat:2,5g.
µg. - Ph:43,4 Na:22,3 Ka:117,79 Mg:18,2 Ca:36,26 Fe:1,83 Zn:0,55 Col.:0 Hsr.:17,98

Quantity of ingredients:
Millet flakes 1 table spoon / 10g. (yes)
Carrot 7/8 lbs / 200g. (yes)
Almond puree 1 teaspoon / 3g. ()
Honey 1/2 teaspoon / 2g. (yes)
Water 1/4 cup / 50g. (yes)

Cooking instructions:
Sprinkle millet flakes with 50 ml of cold water and let it swell for 10 minutes.
Juice the fresh carrots or use 200 ml. carrot juice.
Puree the millet flakes, carrot juice, almond paste and honey with the blender.

9.15 Carrot Risotto

Strengthens immune system, prevents cancer, loss of appetite, flatulence, high blood pressure, depressions, diabetes, diarrhea, stimulates liver function, dissolves stagnation.
Cooking time approx. 45 min
Allergens: GL
2 portions to 340,5g. / 308kcal. - (carb:84% / prot:16%)
100g.=90,46kcal. / protein 8,49g. fat:5,98g.
µg. - Ph:13,57 Na:9,57 Ka:29,14 Mg:16,17 Ca:58,13 Fe:0,33 Zn:0,11 Col.:0,3 Hsr.:7,34

Quantity of ingredients:
Olive oil 1/2 teaspoon / 5g. (yes)
Onion (spring onion) 2 table spoons / 7g. (yes)
Nutmeg 1 pinch / 0,3g. (yes)
Parsley 1/2 bunch / 25g. (yes)
Rice variety any 1/4 lbs - 4oz / 100g. (yes)
Carrot 5/8 lbs - 8oz / 250g. (yes)
Basic recipe for a vegetable soup (nutritious) 1 cup / 280g. (little)
Fennel seeds ground 1/4 teaspoon / 1g. (yes)
Basil (fresh) 1/2 teaspoon / 2g. (yes)
Salt 1 pinch / 1g. (little)
Pepper (ground) 1 pinch / 0,3g. ()
Parmesan 1 table spoon / 10g. ()

Cooking instructions:
Heat the oil in a pan, fry the onions in a glassy and very soft manner.
Add parsley, sauté briefly. Add rice, carrots and nutmeg, sauté briefly
while stirring. Add the vegetable stock, season with fennel and basil,
heat till it boils and cook for about 20 minutes until the rice and carrots
are well. Stir from time to time and add some vegetable stock if
necessary. The risotto should be slightly soupy. Just before the end of
the cooking time mix in the white wine and simmer the risotto for a short
while. Remove risotto from the heat, mix in Parmesan.

9.16 Celery and potato cream soup

Reduces blood pressure, strengthens immune system, promotes weight
loss. Good to fight immunodeficiency, loss of appetite, flatulence,
depressions, diabetes, diarrhea, improves digestion.
Cooking time approx. 45 min
Allergens: GL
4 portions to 241,5g. / 113kcal. - (carb:83% / prot:17%)
100g.=46,69kcal. / protein 2,15g. fat:5,52g.
µg. - Ph:5,96 Na:3,46 Ka:23,98 Mg:22,27 Ca:83,51 Fe:0,18 Zn:0,01 Col.:0 Hsr.:1,49

Quantity of ingredients:
Olive oil 1 table spoon / 10g. (yes)
Onion white 1/2 piece / 25g. (yes)
Basic recipe for a vegetable soup (nutritious) 3 cups / 700g. (little)
Potato 5/8 oz / 200g. (little)
Nutmeg 1 pinch / 0,5g. (yes)
Ground 1 pinch / 0,5g. (yes)

Lemon peel 1/4 piece / 1g. (yes)
Crème fraiche cheese 2 table spoons / 20g. (little)
Salt 1 pinch / 1g. (little)
Parsley 1 table spoon / 8g. (yes)

Cooking instructions:
Heat the olive oil in a saucepan lightly. Fry the onions very gently in a mild heat. Pour with vegetable stock according to the basic recipe. Cover and cook for 15 minutes.
Add curd-cut potato, celery, nutmeg, cumin and lemon zest. Spice with salt and cook for 12 minutes. Potatoes and celery should be soft. Remove the lemon peel.
Puree the soup with crème fraiche using a blender. Season the soup with salt.
Arrange the soup in portions with the chopped parsley.

9.17 Champignon rice

Strengthens kidney, diuretic, warming the body from the inside, expands blood vessels, strengthens the muscles, promotes digestion and is good to fight high blood pressure, dissolves stagnation, promotes weight loss. Good to fight immunodeficiency, loss of appetite.
Cooking time approx. 30 min
Allergens: L
2 portions to 341g. / 410kcal. - (carb:89% / prot:11%)
100g.=120,23kcal. / protein 10,01g. fat:3,44g.
µg. - Ph:30,31 Na:3,54 Ka:32,26 Mg:27,24 Ca:62,74 Fe:0,37 Zn:0,16 Col.:0 Hsr.:12,22

Quantity of ingredients:
Onion white 1 piece / 50g. (yes)
Bay leaf 2 pieces / 1g. (yes)
Clove 2 pieces / 1g. (yes)
Basic recipe for a vegetable soup (nutritious) 7/8 lbs / 350g. (little)
Rice (whole grain) 5/8 oz / 200g. (yes)
Champignon 1/8 lbs - 2oz / 60g. (little)
Parsley 1/2 oz / 20g. (yes)
Pepper (ground) 1 pinch / 0,2g. ()

Cooking instructions:
Plug in the cloves in the onion. Heat the vegetable stock with the onion and the bay leaves till it boils. Add the rice to the boiling liquid, reduce the temperature to the lowest level and stir with the lid closed for 20-25 minutes.

In the meantime, wash the mushrooms, clean them, slice them, sauté briefly with a little water or sauté. Wash the parsley and chop finely. Remove the onion from the rice, add the mushrooms and the parsley, season with pepper.

9.18 Champignon salad with cress

Promotes digestion and is good to fight high blood pressure. Good to fight loss of appetite, improves blood circulation.
Cooking time approx. 5 min
Allergens: AN
1 portion to 312g. / 220kcal. - (carb:56% / prot:44%)
100g.=70,51kcal. / protein 9,74g. fat:7,08g.
µg. - Ph:105,24 Na:37,35 Ka:366,67 Mg:14,25 Ca:19,03 Fe:1,08 Zn:0,41 Col.:0,02
Hsr.:60,22

Quantity of ingredients:
Champignon 5/8 lbs - 8oz / 250g. (little)
Sesame oil 2 table spoons / 6g. (little)
Pepper (ground) 1 pinch / 0,5g. ()
Salt 1 pinch / 1g. (little)
Lemon 1/2 piece / 15g. (yes)
Peppers powder 2 pinches / 0,1g. (little)
Cress 2 table spoons / 10g. (yes)
White bread (wheat bread) 2 slices / 30g. (yes)

Cooking instructions:
Cut mushrooms into thin slices.
Dressing: sesame oil, a little ground pepper, salt, plenty of lemon juice, stir well the rose pepper; give over the finely chopped mushrooms; plenty of watercress.
Goes well with: white bread, round grain rice or quinoa; Along with the cereal, the salad makes a simple, light meal.
Serve with white bread.

9.19 Chicory salad with tangerine

Dissolves mucus, is rich in A-B-C Vitamins, promotes digestion, forcing spleen, promotes weight loss. Good to fight loss
of appetite, flatulence, immunodeficiency.
Cooking time approx. 10 min
Allergens: AGNO
3 portions to 285g. / 257kcal. - (carb:75% / prot:25%)
100g.=90,06kcal. / protein 5,49g. fat:7,73g.
µg. - Ph:2,87 Na:5,09 Ka:18,76 Mg:1,33 Ca:3,14 Fe:0,04 Zn:0,01 Col.:0 Hsr.:2,36

Quantity of ingredients:
Tangerine 4 pieces / 300g. (little)
Chicory 2-3 pieces / 300g. (yes)
Sesame oil 2 table spoons / 18g. (little)
Pepper (ground) 1 pinch / 0,5g. ()
Salt 1 pinch / 1g. (little)
Vinegar Aceto Balsamico 2 teaspoons / 6g. (yes)
Lemon 1/2 piece / 25g. (yes)
Orange 1/2 piece / 70g. (little)
Peppers powder 1 pinch / 1g. (little)
Orange jam 1 teaspoon / 4g. (little)
Cream, sweet 30% 1 table spoon / 10g. (little)
White bread (wheat bread) 6 slices / 120g. (yes)

Cooking instructions:
Peel tangerines and cut into bite-sized pieces; Cut chicory roughly and mix well.
Dressing: sesame oil, pepper, salt, raspberry vinegar or balsamic vinegar, a little lemon or orange juice, rose paprika, orange marmalade or, alternatively, another jam, stir well. Give a little sweet cream over the salad and let it pass briefly.

9.20 Coconut rice with cardamom

Nourishing and slightly warming. Diuretic, reduces blood glucose. Supports urination. Stimulates liver function, detoxifying. Good to fight depressions.
Cooking time approx. 45 min
Allergens: GO
4 portions to 245,25g. / 266kcal. - (carb:66% / prot:34%)
100g.=108,56kcal. / protein 3,82g. fat:12,99g.
µg. - Ph:3,93 Na:0,39 Ka:8,97 Mg:2 Ca:1,15 Fe:0,04 Zn:0,02 Col.:0,31 Hsr.:1,18

Quantity of ingredients:
Rice long grain rice 1 cup / 120g. (yes)
Water 6 cups / 400g. (yes)
Sugar cane sugar 1 table spoon / 10g. (yes)
Cardamom 1 teaspoon / 2g. (little)
Ginger fresh 1/2 teaspoon / 2g. (yes)
Butter organic 2 table spoons / 20g. (yes)
Coconut grated 2 table spoons / 16g. (yes)

Cashews 1 table spoon / 8g. (little)
Raisins 1 table spoon / 8g. ()
Salt 1 pinch / 0,5g. (little)
Lemon 1/2 piece / 15g. (yes)
Pumpkin 3/4 lbs / 300g. (yes)
Olive oil 2 table spoons / 20g. (yes)
Coriander 1 pinch / 0,2g. (yes)
Pepper (ground) 1 pinch / 0,2g. ()
Curry 1 pinch / 0,5g. (yes)
Water 1/4 cup / 50g. (yes)
Salt 1 pinch / 0,5g. (little)
Parsley 1 table spoon / 8g. (yes)
Cardamom 1 pinch / 0,2g. (little)
Turmeric (yellow root) 1 pinch / 0,2g. (little)

Cooking instructions:
Preparation: Soak long grain rice in cold water for 1 hour and drain.

Then: Heat fresh water till it boils; add some whole cane sugar, plenty of ground cardamom or some cardamom pods, grated ginger and the rice into the hot water and cook.

Separately: heat some butter in a hot pot; add grated coconut, cashews and raisins; add the cooked rice and salt; pour lemon juice over it; mix everything and let it pass for a few minutes.

Pumpkin vegetables: heat olive oil in a pan. Steam the pumpkin (cut in cubes), season with cilantro, pepper and curry, simmer with a little water, salt with sea salt, add chopped parsley with cardamom and turmeric, simmer on a small fire for about 10 minutes, depending on the pumpkin, the pumpkin should still be firm.

9.21 Cold cherry soup with curd cheese dumpling

Improves blood circulation, reduces inflammation, good to fight weakness, belching, diabetes, acute or chronic obstruction of the bowel. Laxative, stimulates digestion, cleans the intestinal flora.
Cooking time approx. 2 hours and more
Allergens: GO
2 portions to 307g. / 320kcal. - (carb:70% / prot:30%)
100g.=104,23kcal. / protein 7,97g. fat:15,18g.
µg. - Ph:12,34 Na:3,16 Ka:31,13 Mg:2,66 Ca:11,16 Fe:0,08 Zn:0,05 Col.:1,51 Hsr.:2,44

Quantity of ingredients:
Cherry compote 7/8 lbs / 450g. (little)
Agar agar (kelp) 1/2 teaspoon / 1,5g. (yes)
Curd cheese 20% 1/4 lbs - 4oz / 100g. (little)
Sour cream 15% fat 1/8 lbs - 2oz / 50g. (little)
Vanilla sugar natural 1 package / 1g. (yes)
Sugar brown 1 table spoon / 10g. (yes)
Cinnamon ground 1 pinch / 0,5g. (little)
Lemon peel 1 pinch / 1g. (yes)

Cooking instructions:
Strain the cherry compote.
Finely puree half of the cherries with the cherry juice using a blender and pass through a sieve.
Stir agar agar powder with cold water until smooth.
Bring the cherry puree to boil while stirring.
Mix in the agar-agar and cook the cherry puree for 1 minute while stirring.
Spread hot cherry puree on two soup plates.
Sprinkle the remaining cherries into the soup.
Cool down cherry soup for 2 hours until lightly gelled.
Use the hand mixer to stir the cord cheese, sour cream, sugar, vanilla sugar, cinnamon and lemon zest into a smooth, firm cream.
From the cream with the tablespoon, prick small dumplings and put them into the cherry soup.

9.22 Cucumber salad

Diuretic, detoxifying, suppresses conversion of sugar into fat, lowers cholesterol, prevents cancer. Cucumber cools and moistens. Dill works against flatulence, anticonvulsant in gastrointestinal discomfort.
Cooking time approx. 5 min
Allergens: O
2 portions to 206g. / 27kcal. - (carb:68% / prot:32%)
100g.=13,11kcal. / protein 1,61g. fat:0,4g.
µg. - Ph:5,92 Na:2,32 Ka:35,15 Mg:2,16 Ca:4,03 Fe:0,12 Zn:0,05 Col.:0 Hsr.:1,94

Quantity of ingredients:
Cucumber 1 piece / 400g. (yes)
Salt 1 pinch / 1g. (little)
Dill 1 pinch / 1g. (yes)
Vinegar (Apple vinegar) 1 table spoon / 10g. (yes)

Cooking instructions:
Cut the cucumber (do not peel the BIO) thinly and season.

9.23 Cucumber soup

Diuretic, detoxifying, suppresses conversion of sugar into fat, lowers cholesterol, prevents cancer, promotes digestion, diaphoretic, dries out, good to fight yeast infections.
Cooking time approx. 20 min
Allergens: M
4 portions to 235,25g. / 96kcal. - (carb:22% / prot:78%)
100g.=40,6kcal. / protein 0,91g. fat:9,03g.
µg. - Ph:2,67 Na:1,28 Ka:15,6 Mg:1,17 Ca:2,57 Fe:0,06 Zn:0,01 Col.:0 Hsr.:0,85

Quantity of ingredients:
Olive oil 2 table spoons / 35g. (yes)
Cucumber 2 pieces / 400g. (yes)
Water 2 cup / 500g. (yes)
Sage 3 leaves / 3g. (yes)
Mustard 1/2 teaspoon / 0,5g. (little)
Coriander 1 pinch / 1g. (yes)
Cardamom 1 pinch / 1g. (little)
Salt 1 pinch / 1g. (little)

Cooking instructions:
Heat oil and roast short the small cucumbers. Add Mustard seeds, coriander, cardamom and salt. Add water. Simmer for 10-15 min. Puree and decorate with fresh chopped sage.

9.24 Delicately spiced zucchini with tomatoes

Diuretic, promotes digestion, helps to digest fat, reduces blood pressure, dissolves stagnation, antioxidative, supports urination, diuretic, warming the body from the inside, expands blood vessels.
Cooking time approx. 10 min
4 portions to 396,5g. / 203kcal. - (carb:72% / prot:28%)
100g.=51,2kcal. / protein 5,38g. fat:6,62g.
µg. - Ph:10,4 Na:0,79 Ka:35,33 Mg:6,3 Ca:5,58 Fe:0,26 Zn:0,02 Col.:0 Hsr.:5,53

Quantity of ingredients:
Olive oil 1 table spoon / 20g. (yes)
Onion white 2 pieces / 120g. (yes)
Zucchini 4 pieces / 800g. (yes)
Oregano dried 1 pinch / 1g. (yes)
Basil (fresh) 6-8 leaves / 3g. (yes)

Salt 1 pinch / 1g. (little)
Tomato 2 pieces / 120g. (yes)
Rice (whole grain) 1 cup / 120g. (yes)
Water 6 cups / 400g. (yes)
Salt 1 pinch / 1g. (little)

Cooking instructions:
In a hot pan, fry olive oil, finely chopped onions and finely chopped zucchini until half cooked. Add plenty of dried oregano. Salt and chop the tomatoes for a few minutes until the zucchini are tender but crisp. Add fresh basil as desired.

Variation: Put some sheep's cheese over the tomatoes and finish cooking with the lid closed.

Place the rice in salted water, heat till it boils and let it simmer over low heat for about 15 minutes.

9.25 Fennel-Rice Soup

Forcing spleen, relieves constipation, stimulates nerves, detoxifying, reduces inflammation, improves blood circulation.
Cooking time approx. 15-20 min
Allergens: EG
2 portions to 234g. / 156kcal. - (carb:88% / prot:12%)
100g.=66,45kcal. / protein 3,57g. fat:6,64g.
µg. - Ph:7,34 Na:16,24 Ka:41,07 Mg:52,9 Ca:55,34 Fe:0,27 Zn:0,06 Col.:1,92 Hsr.:2,45

Quantity of ingredients:
Basic recipe for a rice soup (Congee) 1 cup / 300g. (little)
Fennel 1/2 piece / 150g. (yes)
Butter organic 1 table spoon / 15g. (yes)
Soy sauce 1 dash / 3g. (little)

Cooking instructions:
Cook the fennel softly in the rice soup according to the basic recipe. Before serving, add a piece of butter and some soy sauce.

9.26 Frozen pineapple juice

Pineapple reduce inflammation, supports urination, cleans the skin.
Cooking time approx. 1 1/2 hours
1 portion to 50g. / 29kcal. - (carb:95% / prot:5%)
100g.=58kcal. / protein 0,25g. fat:0,1g.
µg. - Ph:9 Na:2 Ka:173 Mg:17 Ca:16 Fe:0,4 Zn:0,3 Col.:0 Hsr.:7

Quantity of ingredients:
Pineapple 1/8 lbs - 2oz / 50g. (little)

Cooking instructions:
Juice pineapple yourself or freeze the organic pineapple juice in small portions and if necessary suck.

9.27 Fruit juice

Stops diarrhea, promotes digestion, appetizing, harmonizes the stomach, relieves pain, detoxifying, reduces blood pressure, strengthens immune system, prevents cancer, reduces radiation damage.
Cooking time approx. 10 min
2 portions to 305g. / 176kcal. - (carb:93% / prot:7%)
100g.=57,54kcal. / protein 1,89g. fat:0,9g.
µg. - Ph:4,99 Na:2,24 Ka:37,45 Mg:2,36 Ca:6,04 Fe:0,21 Zn:0,05 Col.:0 Hsr.:4,3

Quantity of ingredients:
Orange 2 pieces / 150g. (little)
Apple (sweet) 4 pieces / 300g. (little)
Carrot 2 pieces / 150g. (yes)
Honey 1 table spoon / 10g. (yes)

Cooking instructions:
Peel oranges and carrots. Cut all ingredients into cubes so that they fit into the juicer and juice. Sweet with honey.

9.28 Grapefruit juice

Promotes digestion, lowers blood glucose, dries out, provides Vitamin C
Cooking time approx. 5 min
1 portion to 250g. / 107kcal. - (carb:92% / prot:8%)
100g.=42,8kcal. / protein 1,5g. fat:0,5g.
µg. - Ph:17 Na:2 Ka:180 Mg:10 Ca:18 Fe:0,3 Zn:0,2 Col.:0 Hsr.:15

Quantity of ingredients:
Grapefruit (Pomelo) 1 cup / 250g. (yes)

Cooking instructions:
Juice fresh grapefruit or use organic juice.

9.29 Grated apple

Eat 3 times a day - Apple (sour) scraped and brown is stuffing. Relieves
diarrhea.
Cooking time approx. 10 min
1 portion to 200g. / 120kcal. - (carb:94% / prot:6%)
100g.=60kcal. / protein 0,6g. fat:0,8g.
µg. - Ph:11 Na:3 Ka:144 Mg:6 Ca:7 Fe:0,5 Zn:0,1 Col.:0 Hsr.:15

Quantity of ingredients:
Apple (sour) 1 piece / 200g. (little)

Cooking instructions:
Peel apple and grate as fine as possible. Leave for at least 5 minutes
until it turns brown.

9.30 Hearty polenta mash

Strengths spleen and stomach, promotes watering, promotes digestion,
detoxifying, promotes perspiration, reduces blood lipids, stimulates,
dissolves stagnation, stimulates appetite, dissolves stagnation.
Cooking time approx. 10 min
2 portions to 207,5g. / 262kcal. - (carb:80% / prot:20%)
100g.=126,27kcal. / protein 5,65g. fat:5,94g.
µg. - Ph:6,71 Na:0,73 Ka:11,2 Mg:2,2 Ca:2,17 Fe:0,09 Zn:0,05 Col.:0 Hsr.:2,46

Quantity of ingredients:
Corn Grease (Polenta) 1 cup / 120g. (yes)
Onion (spring onion) 2 pieces / 40g. (yes)
Ginger fresh 1/2 teaspoon / 2g. (yes)
Nutmeg 1 pinch / 1g. (yes)
Salt 1 pinch / 1g. (little)
Olive oil 1 table spoon / 10g. (yes)
Turmeric (yellow root) 1 pinch / 1g. (little)
Water 1 1/2 cups / 240g. (yes)

Cooking instructions:
Stir in the polenta in boiling water and let it swell for 7 min. Add green onion, grated ginger, turmeric, nutmeg, salt and olive oil and wait for 3 more minutes.

9.31 Kohlrabi in chervil sauce with potatoes

Reduces inflammation, lowers cholesterol, diuretic, conducts bowel winds, strengthens immune system, prevents cancer, promotes weight loss. Good to fight loss of appetite, flatulence, high blood pressure, depressions, diabetes, diarrhea.
Cooking time approx. 1 hour
Allergens: GL
4 portions to 316,75g. / 188kcal. - (carb:79% / prot:21%)
100g.=59,19kcal. / protein 8,66g. fat:2,51g.
µg. - Ph:2,95 Na:1,03 Ka:25,06 Mg:3,48 Ca:15,16 Fe:0,04 Zn:0,02 Col.:0,06 Hsr.:0,91

Quantity of ingredients:
Potato 6 pieces / 450g. (little)
Basic recipe for a vegetable soup (nutritious) 1 cup / 300g. (little)
Potato 1/4 lbs - 4oz / 100g. (little)
Nutmeg 1 pinch / 0,2g. (yes)
Lemon peel 1/2 teaspoon / 2g. (yes)
Ginger fresh 1/2 teaspoon / 2g. (yes)
Lovage 1/2 teaspoon / 2g. (yes)
Kohlrabi 3/4 lbs / 300g. (little)
Salt 1 pinch / 1g. (little)
Pepper (ground) 1 pinch / 0,2g. ()
Sour cream 15% fat 3 table spoons / 30g. (little)
Chervil dried 1 Bunch / 80g. (yes)

Cooking instructions:
Boil the potatoes in salted water. Bring half of the vegetable stock to boil. Add the diced potatoes, nutmeg, lemon zest, ginger and lovage. Cover the potatoes and cook for about 10 minutes until soft and puree them with a blender until they are smooth.
Bring remaining vegetable stock to boil. Cut kohlrabi into cubes and add, cover and cook for about 8 minutes. Stir in the potato sauce and heat everything briefly.
Puree with the mixing stick chervil and sour cream. Mix the chervil cream with the kohlrabi vegetables.
Serve with the cooked, peeled potatoes.

9.32 Lasagne with tofu cream

Harmonizes spleen and stomach, reduces Flatulence, protects the digestive system. Good to fight lack of appetite, flatulence, inflammatory bowel disease, stomach ulcers, rheumatism, heartburn, twelffinger intestinal ulcers.
Cooking time approx. 45 min
Allergens: ACEG
4 portions to 231g. / 301kcal. - (carb:50% / prot:50%)
100g.=130,3kcal. / protein 19,33g. fat:11,88g.
µg. - Ph:8,79 Na:3,51 Ka:7,05 Mg:4,06 Ca:7,27 Fe:0,09 Zn:0,05 Col.:3,83 Hsr.:3,82

Quantity of ingredients:
Soy Tofu 7/8 lbs / 400g. (little)
Chicken egg 2 pieces / 100g. (yes)
Onion white 2 pieces / 120g. (yes)
Tomato 1/4 lbs - 4oz / 100g. (yes)
Oregano dried 1 pinch / 1g. (yes)
Marjoram 1 pinch / 1g. (yes)
Peppers powder 1 pinch / 1g. (little)
Salt 1 pinch / 1g. (little)
Noodles (wheat, lasagne) with egg 3/8 lbs - 6oz / 150g. (rec.)
Edam cheese 1/8 lbs - 2oz / 50g. (little)

Cooking instructions:
Tofu cream: Mix tofu with eggs, onions, small tomatoes, oregano, marjoram, peppers and some sea salt put into a smooth mass using a kitchen machine with a knife or a blender.
Lasagne: Place 1/5 of the tofu cream in a casserole dish (25x15cm), cover with 3 lasagna leaves, repeat this process twice, and then finish the last fifth of the tofu cream over the pastry plates. Sprinkle with a little grated Edam and bake in the oven at 175°C/347°F for about 1/2 hour.

9.33 Lentil and chestnut soup with curry

Reduces blood pressure, strengthens immune system, prevents cancer, reduces radiation damage, forcing spleen, dissolves stagnation, promotes weight loss. Good to fight immunodeficiency, loss of appetite, flatulence, high blood pressure, depressions, diabetes, diarrhea.
Cooking time approx. 45 min
Allergens: LO
4 portions to 238,25g. / 175kcal. - (carb:83% / prot:17%)
100g.=73,45kcal. / protein 4,17g. fat:4,33g.
µg. - Ph:2,67 Na:3,8 Ka:7,98 Mg:4,63 Ca:15,86 Fe:0,06 Zn:0,02 Col.:0 Hsr.:2,07

Quantity of ingredients:
Lentils red 3/8 lbs - 6oz / 150g. (little)
Chestnuts 3/8 lbs - 6oz / 150g. (little)
Olive oil 1 table spoon / 10g. (yes)
Curry 2 teaspoons / 8g. (yes)
Turmeric (yellow root) 1 teaspoon / 2g. (little)
Basic recipe for a vegetable soup (nutritious) 2 cup / 500g. (little)
White wine 1/2 cup / 125g. (little)
Salt (herbal) 1 pinch / 1g. (little)
Anise (Common Fennel) 1 pinch / 1g. (yes)
Cardamom 1 pinch / 0,5g. (little)
Parsley 2 table spoons / 6g. (yes)

Cooking instructions:
Add the olive oil to a pan, sauté the chestnuts, sprinkle with the curry, add the lentils and season with vegetable stock, add a little white wine, mix in the curcuma, simmer for about 20 minutes (until the chestnuts are tender).
Then puree the soup.
Taste with a pinch of anise, cardamom and herbal salt. At the end, sprinkle finely chopped parsley over it.

9.34 Lettuce with fresh cheese

The bitter substances have diuretic effect and promote the blood circulation in the digestive area. Mustard improves thyroid function, relieves rheumatism symptoms.
Cooking time approx. 5 min
Allergens: AFM
1 portion to 260g. / 802kcal. - (carb:21% / prot:79%)
100g.=308,46kcal. / protein 22,11g. fat:52,97g.
µg. - Ph:138,82 Na:313,1 Ka:257,72 Mg:28,88 Ca:84,62 Fe:0,54 Zn:0,48 Col.:0,06 Hsr.:14,65

Quantity of ingredients:
Leaf salads (bitter) 2 portions / 60g. (yes)
Fresh cheese from soya 3/8 lbs - 6oz / 150g. (rec.)
Mustard 1 knife tip / 1g. (little)
Lemon juice 1 dash / 3g. (yes)
Salt 1 pinch / 1g. (little)
Pepper (ground) 1 pinch / 0,5g. ()
Herbs various 2 teaspoons / 4g. (yes)
Black caraway 1 pinch / 1g. (yes)
Whole grain bread 2 slices / 40g. (little)

Cooking instructions:
Wash lettuce and finely pluck.
Mix 150 ml cream cheese, splashes of mustard, splashes of lemon juice, 1 clove of garlic, chopped fresh herbs, pinch of pepper and crushed black cumin and pour over. Serve with wholemeal bread.

9.35 Noodles with meat sauce

Strengthens gastrointestinal function, expands blood vessels, strengthens spleen and stomach, strengthens the muscles, tendons and bones. Relieves fatigue, warms stomach.
Cooking time approx. 2 hours and more
Allergens: ACG
6 portions to 254,17g. / 277kcal. - (carb:23% / prot:77%)
100g.=108,92kcal. / protein 26,54g. fat:13,38g.
µg. - Ph:3,14 Na:0,88 Ka:4,54 Mg:0,66 Ca:0,85 Fe:0,03 Zn:0,06 Col.:0,89 Hsr.:2,34

Quantity of ingredients:
Beef meat (calf) 1,1 lbs / 500g. (little)
Onion white 2 pieces / 120g. (yes)
Water 1 cup / 200g. (yes)
Butter organic 1/8 lbs - 2oz / 50g. (yes)
Peppers powder 1 teaspoon / 3g. (little)
Lettuce 2 pieces / 300g. (yes)
Yogurt (natural, 1.5% fat) 3 table spoons / 30g. (yes)
Cream, sweet 30% 3 table spoons / 30g. (little)
Salt (herbal) 1/2 teaspoon / 2g. (little)
Pepper (ground) 1 pinch / 0,2g. ()
Noodles (whole grain) with egg 5/8 lbs - 8oz / 250g. (rec.)
Salt 1 teaspoon / 4g. (little)
Corn starch 2 teaspoons / 6g. (yes)
Crème fraiche cheese 3 table spoons / 30g. (little)

Cooking instructions:
Free the meat from fat and tendons and dice small.
Peel and chop the onions. Melt half of the butter, fry the onions in it.
Add the water and add the paprika and the meat. Cook over medium
heat for about 2 hours. From time to pour some water.

Clean and wash the salad. (Set aside about 150g. - 3/8 lbs - 6oz heart
leaves for the baby.) Pluck the remaining leaves into bite-sized pieces.

For the salad dressing, mix the yoghurt with 2 tablespoons cream, the
herb salt and the pepper.

Cook the noodles in slightly salted water, then drain.
(When the meat is cooked, remove about 40g - 1/8 lbs - 2oz of meat
and 1 tablespoon of sauce for the baby.)

Salt the goulash, bring to the boil, stir in the cornstarch and bring to the
boil. Stir in the creme fraiche.

(For the baby cut the heart leaves into fine strips and simmer in 1
teaspoon butter, finely puree the meat and the sauce and mix 100 g. -
1/4 lbs - 4oz noodles with 1 teaspoon butter and fill in the baby plate.
Season the salad with 1 tablespoon of cream and serve with the meat.)

For the family, add the remaining butter to the pasta, mix the salad with
the sauce and serve.

9.36 Noodles with vegetable and tomato sauce

Protects the digestive system. Detoxifying, Good to fight loss of
appetite, flatulence, inflammatory bowel disease, obesity, gout, stomach
ulcers, stomach cramps, rheumatism, heartburn, twelffinger intestinal
ulcers, promotes digestion, helps to digest fat.
Cooking time approx. 45 min
Allergens: ACG
2 portions to 281g. / 562kcal. - (carb:70% / prot:30%)
100g.=199,82kcal. / protein 14,06g. fat:21,68g.
µg. - Ph:21,13 Na:3,21 Ka:44,61 Mg:8,06 Ca:6,77 Fe:0,3 Zn:0,2 Col.:8,37 Hsr.:18,02

Quantity of ingredients:
Tomato 1/4 lbs - 4oz / 125g. (yes)
Carrot 1 piece / 80g. (yes)
Zucchini 1 piece / 80g. (yes)

Olive oil 1 table spoon / 15g. (yes)
Onion (shallot) 1 piece / 20g. (yes)
Oregano dried 1 pinch / 1g. (yes)
Salt 1 pinch / 1g. (little)
Pepper (ground) 1 pinch / 0,2g. ()
Noodles (wheat) with egg 5/8 oz / 200g. (rec.)
Olive oil 1 table spoon / 10g. (yes)
Crème fraiche cheese 2 table spoons / 30g. (little)

Cooking instructions:
Boil the tomatoes with a little water, drain and collect the juice, cut the tomatoes into pieces.
Roughly grate zucchini and carrot. Heat olive oil in a pot. Steam shallots very soft. Add tomatoes, season with oregano, salt and pepper. Simmer tomatoes to a thick sauce.
Bring plenty of salted water to boil, cook the wholegrain noodles until firm. In the cooking time of the pasta, heat in a pan olive oil. Fry the carrots while stirring, lightly salt. Add zucchini, sauté briefly while stirring. The vegetables should be soft with a bite.
Drain pasta, mix with crème fraiche, season with salt and pepper. Garnish with the tomato sauce.

9.37 Oat Congee

Strengthens immune system.
Cooking time approx. 2-4 hours
Allergens: A
3 portions to 275g. / 162kcal. - (carb:74% / prot:26%)
100g.=58,91kcal. / protein 7,04g. fat:2,87g.
µg. - Ph:5,76 Na:0,23 Ka:5,98 Mg:2,27 Ca:1,82 Fe:0,1 Zn:0,08 Col.:0 Hsr.:2,51

Quantity of ingredients:
Oat 1 cup / 125g. (yes)
Water 6 cups / 700g. (yes)

Cooking instructions:
Cook oats and water in a ratio of about 1: 6. The amount of water determines the thickness of the mash (pure matter of taste). The oats swell, so do not take much. Put the oats in a saucepan with good insulation and a heavy lid. It is important to simmer the oats after a short boil on the slightest flame, otherwise it burns. Cook the oat for 2-4 hours. The longer it cooks, the more he strengthens.

9.38 Oatmeal soup with spring onion and carrots

Reduces blood pressure, strengthens immune system, prevents cancer, reduces radiation damage, stimulates digestion, reduces pain, stimulates appetite, dissolves stagnation.
Cooking time approx. 30 min
Allergens: AG
3 portions to 266,33g. / 135kcal. - (carb:65% / prot:35%)
100g.=50,56kcal. / protein 3,87g. fat:5,59g.
µg. - Ph:3,67 Na:1,03 Ka:7,89 Mg:1,41 Ca:2,55 Fe:0,1 Zn:0,05 Col.:0,5 Hsr.:1,63

Quantity of ingredients:
Oat 6 table spoons / 48g. (yes)
Carrot 2 pieces / 200g. (yes)
Butter organic 1 table spoon / 15g. (yes)
Nutmeg 1 pinch / 1g. (yes)
Lovage 1 stem / 15g. (yes)
Onion (spring onion) 2 pieces / 40g. (yes)
Water 2 cup / 480g. (yes)

Cooking instructions:
Roast the oats in butter, add salt and spices, pour in water and heat till it boils. After 10 min. add the grated carrots and lovage, cook for 10 minutes. Finely add chopped onion.

9.39 Paprika turkey with rice and lettuce

Strengthens blood and bone marrow.
Cooking time approx. 1 hour
Allergens: AG
6 portions to 360,67g. / 391kcal. - (carb:23% / prot:77%)
100g.=108,5kcal. / protein 32,56g. fat:36,94g.
µg. - Ph:3,05 Na:0,65 Ka:3,68 Mg:0,58 Ca:0,79 Fe:0,03 Zn:0,01 Col.:0,91 Hsr.:2,44

Quantity of ingredients:
Olive oil 2 table spoons / 20g. (yes)
Onion white 1 piece / 60g. (yes)
Peppers (rose peppers) 2 table spoons / 14g. (yes)
Chicken meat 1 piece / 800g. (yes)
Water 1 cup / 250g. (yes)
Salt 1 pinch / 1g. (little)
Spelled wholemeal flour 1 table spoon / 7g. (little)
Sour cream 15% fat 5/8 lbs - 8oz / 250g. (little)
Water 6 cups / 400g. (yes)
Rice Basmati 1 cup / 120g. (yes)

Salt 1 pinch / 1g. (little)
Lettuce 1 piece / 200g. (yes)
Olive oil 2 table spoons / 20g. (yes)
Lemon juice 1/2 piece / 15g. (yes)
Herbs various 2 table spoons / 6g. (yes)

Cooking instructions:
Heat the oil in a saucepan and fry the onions in a golden yellow.
Sprinkle plenty of peppers over the onion and stir well so that it does
not burn. Put the pot aside.
In a casserole, fry the chicken parts from one side; turn the meat over,
spread the onion above and fry the chicken parts from the other side.
As soon as they have taken on a deep red color, pour the vegetable
broth and heat till it boils.
Season with salt, reduce the heat and stew the chicken for 45 minutes
or until cooked.
Put the poultry parts together with cooking liquid in a bowl and set
aside.
Add 2 to 3 tbsp of flour to the casserole and gradually add the cooking
solution again, stirring constantly until the sauce is thickened.
Stir in the sour cream or yoghurt, put the poultry pieces back into the
pot and heat again well, but do not boil.
Place the rice with the salted water, bring to the boil and simmer until
the rice is tender.
Wash and dry the lettuce. Pluck small and put in a bowl.
In a cup, mix the olive oil, the lemon juice, the salt and fresh chopped
herbs and pour over the salad.

9.40 Paprika-tomato rice

Good to fight little cholesterol, diabetes. Low in protein, low fat content,
little protein. Forcing spleen, dissolves stagnation, promotes weight
loss. Good to fight immunodeficiency, loss of appetite, flatulence, high
blood pressure, depressions.
Cooking time approx. 25 min
Allergens: L
3 portions to 324g. / 291kcal. - (carb:89% / prot:11%)
100g.=89,92kcal. / protein 7,63g. fat:2,54g.
µg. - Ph:10,3 Na:1,31 Ka:15,5 Mg:9,5 Ca:22,5 Fe:0,14 Zn:0,06 Col.:0 Hsr.:4,12

Quantity of ingredients:
Onion white 1 piece / 50g. (yes)
Peppers 4 pieces / 120g. (yes)
Bay leaf 2 pieces / 1g. (yes)
Clove 2 pieces / 1g. (yes)
Basic recipe for a vegetable soup (nutritious) 7/8 lbs / 400g. (little)
Rice (whole grain) 5/8 oz / 200g. (yes)
Champignon 1/8 lbs - 2oz / 60g. (little)
Parsley 1/2 oz / 20g. (yes)
Pepper (ground) 1 pinch / 0,2g. ()
Peppers (rose peppers) 1 pinch / 0,2g. (yes)
Tomato 1/4 lbs - 4oz / 120g. (yes)

Cooking instructions:
Finely chop the onion. Cut the peppers into fine strips.
Heat margarine in a saucepan, sauté onions and peppers, and rice.
Add the vegetable stock, add cloves and bay leaves and leave to
simmer in a closed pot for approx. 20 minutes. Cut the tomato meat into
1 cm cubes and add to the rice 5 minutes before the end of cooking.

9.41 Pear juice

Promotes digestion, supports urination.
Cooking time approx. 5 min
2 portions to 300g. / 180kcal. - (carb:93% / prot:7%)
100g.=60kcal. / protein 1,8g. fat:1,2g.
µg. - Ph:7,5 Na:1 Ka:62,5 Mg:3,5 Ca:4,5 Fe:0,15 Zn:0,05 Col.:0 Hsr.:7,5

Quantity of ingredients:
Pear 3 pieces / 600g. (little)

Cooking instructions:
Peel pears thinly (vitamins under the skin) and core. Juice in the juicer.

9.42 Polenta with peach

Relieves fatigue, forcing spleen, diuretic, strengthens the defense, good
to fight fungi infections, lets urine and bile juice flow, prevents the aging
process, strengthens brain cells.
Cooking time approx. 20 min
3 portions to 254g. / 197kcal. - (carb:89% / prot:11%)
100g.=77,56kcal. / protein 4,48g. fat:0,6g.
µg. - Ph:2,76 Na:0,12 Ka:11,83 Mg:0,93 Ca:1,02 Fe:0,05 Zn:0,02 Col.:0 Hsr.:1,56

Quantity of ingredients:
Water 1 1/2 cups / 240g. (yes)
Corn Grease (Polenta) 1 cup / 120g. (yes)
Peaches 2-3 pieces / 400g. (little)
Vanilla pod 1 pinch / 1g. (yes)
Chili (pod or ground) 1 pinch / 0,1g. (yes)
Cinnamon ground 1 pinch / 1g. (little)

Cooking instructions:
Pour the polenta into a pan of hot water with constant stirring until the polenta has the desired consistency. Pull the
polenta from the fire and let it soak for 10 minutes.
Wash fresh peaches and cut into quarters. Pour into the finished polenta the peaches, add the vanilla and add Chili
to taste, stir and let it go for 3 minutes.
Winter varieties: Pickled fruit, pear, apples.

9.43 Polenta with ratatouille

Forcing spleen and stomach, lets urine and bile juice flow. Diuretic, supports urination. Promotes digestion, helps to digest fat, supports urination, reduces blood pressure.
Cooking time approx. 30 min
Allergens: G
4 portions to 360,75g. / 226kcal. - (carb:66% / prot:34%)
100g.=62,51kcal. / protein 7,77g. fat:7,86g.
µg. - Ph:2,23 Na:1,22 Ka:9,69 Mg:0,92 Ca:2,28 Fe:0,05 Zn:0,02 Col.:0,07 Hsr.:0,97

Quantity of ingredients:
Corn Grease (Polenta) 1 cup / 120g. (yes)
Water 1 1/2 cups / 240g. (yes)
Aubergine 1 piece (large) / 200g. (yes)
Zucchini 2 pieces / 500g. (yes)
Onion white 2 pieces / 120g. (yes)
Tomato 2 pieces (blended) / 200g. (yes)
Olive oil 2 table spoons / 20g. (yes)
Salt 1 pinch / 0,5g. (little)
Parsley 1 table spoon (chopped) / 8g. (yes)
Thyme 1/2 teaspoon / 1g. (yes)
Onion (spring onion) 2 table spoons (chopped) / 12g. (yes)
Basil 4 leaves / 2g. (yes)
Parmesan 2 table spoons / 20g. ()

Cooking instructions:
Use double the amount of water to polenta, add salt and oil and heat till it boils. Stir in polenta, stirring constantly. Take off the fire and let it swell for 20 minutes. Meanwhile, cut the onion, fry in a saucepan with hot oil. Add the diced zucchini, tomatoes and melanzani and simmer for about 20 minutes. Add basil, thyme, salt.
Coat baking tray with oil, apply polenta evenly and wait until it gets stronger.
Add the cooked ratatouille to polenta, portion and then put in the oven for a few minutes (possibly with grated parmesan).
Sprinkle with fresh parsley and finely chopped spring onion.
The valuable tip: The Polenta sections are ideal for on the go.

9.44 Potato gnocchi with vegetables and basil sauce

Strengthens immune system, promotes weight loss. Good to fight immunodeficiency, loss of appetite, flatulence, high blood pressure. Relaxing and reassuring.
Cooking time approx. 1 hour
Allergens: ACGL
4 portions to 290,25g. / 167kcal. - (carb:75% / prot:25%)
100g.=57,45kcal. / protein 6,54g. fat:4,63g.
µg. - Ph:3,26 Na:1,11 Ka:13,57 Mg:2,45 Ca:9,39 Fe:0,06 Zn:0,02 Col.:1,36 Hsr.:1,49

Quantity of ingredients:
Potato 5/8 lbs - 8oz / 250g. (little)
Wheat flour 1 oz / 25g. (yes)
Wheat semolina 1/2 oz / 15g. (yes)
Chicken yolk 1 piece / 20g. (yes)
Nutmeg 1 pinch / 0,2g. (yes)
Basic recipe for a vegetable soup (nutritious) 1 cup / 250g. (little)
Celery root 1/8 lbs - 2oz / 50g. (yes)
Lemon peel 1/2 teaspoon / 2g. (yes)
Ginger fresh 1/2 teaspoon / 2g. (yes)
Nutmeg 1 pinch / 0,2g. (yes)
Basil (fresh) 1 Bunch / 125g. (yes)
Crème fraiche cheese 1 table spoon / 20g. (little)
Salt 1 pinch / 1g. (little)
Pepper (ground) 1 pinch / 0,2g. ()
Carrot 1/4 lbs - 4oz / 100g. (yes)
Zucchini 1/4 lbs - 4oz / 100g. (yes)
Cauliflower 1/4 lbs - 4oz / 100g. (yes)
Broccoli 1/4 lbs - 4oz / 100g. (little)
Salt 1 pinch / 1g. (little)

Cooking instructions:
Steam the potatoes gently, peel and pass hot through the potato press. Process the hot potatoes with flour, semolina, egg, nutmeg and salt to a smooth dough. Let dough rest for 3o minutes.
Make small rolls (2 cm) out of the dough with flour-dusted hands, cut off 1 cm thin slices. To create the typical gnocchi shape, gently dab the dough pieces with your thumb. Leave the gnocchi in lightly boiling salted water for 6 - 8 minutes. Lift the gnocchi out of the pot with the skimmer.

Heat the vegetable stock till it boils. Add diced celery, grated lemon peel, finely chopped ginger and 1 pinch of nutmeg. Cover and simmer for about 10 minutes. Using the blender, puree the vegetable broth, celery, chopped basil and créme fraiche into a smooth sauce. Season with salt and nutmeg.

Cut carrots, zucchini, cauliflower and broccoli into small pieces and cook covered in a sieve over steam for 8 minutes until firm.
Heat the sauce again and add to the vegetables and arrange over the gnocchi.

9.45 Potato with dandelion salad

Promotes spleen, reduces inflammation, improves digestion, regenerates skin, supports urinating, lowers cholesterol, detoxifying, reduces inflammation, forcing spleen and digestive system, detoxifying, dissolves stagnation.
Cooking time approx. 25 min
2 portions to 203g. / 162kcal. - (carb:70% / prot:30%)
100g.=79,8kcal. / protein 4,28g. fat:5,59g.
µg. - Ph:26,58 Na:13,03 Ka:176,11 Mg:11,88 Ca:27,41 Fe:0,61 Zn:0,28 Col.:0,01
Hsr.:14,22

Quantity of ingredients:
Potato 5/8 lbs - 8oz / 250g. (little)
Onion white 1/2 piece / 20g. (yes)
Sunflower oil 1 table spoon / 10g. (little)
Dandelion (young plants) 1/4 lbs - 4oz / 125g. (yes)
Salt 1 pinch / 1g. (little)
Pepper white (ground) 1 pinch / 0,5g. (yes)

Cooking instructions:
Cook the potatoes in salted water and cut into thin slices. Finely chop the onion. Now season the potatoes with oil, salt and pepper and add the dandelion and mix.

9.46 Pumpkin curry

Promotes digestion and sweating, Dissolves stagnation, strengthens lungs and spleen, diuretic, reduces blood glucose, forcing spleen and digestive system, detoxifying, strengthens the muscles and bones. Cooking time approx. 20 min

3 portions to 251g. / 193kcal. - (carb:63% / prot:37%)
100g.=77,03kcal. / protein 2,72g. fat:10,61g.
µg. - Ph:5,14 Na:0,86 Ka:16,34 Mg:2,68 Ca:2,29 Fe:0,06 Zn:0,02 Col.:0 Hsr.:1,54

Quantity of ingredients:
Pumpkin 3/4 lbs / 300g. (yes)
Olive oil 2 table spoons / 30g. (yes)
Coriander 1 pinch / 1g. (yes)
Pepper (ground) 1 pinch / 0,5g. ()
Curry 1 pinch / 1g. (yes)
Water 1/4 cup / 50g. (yes)
Salt 1 pinch / 1g. (little)
Parsley 1 table spoon / 7g. (yes)
Cardamom 1 pinch / 1g. (little)
Turmeric (yellow root) 1 pinch / 1g. (little)
Rice (whole grain) 1/2 cup / 60g. (yes)
Water 3 cups / 300g. (yes)
Salt 1 pinch / 1g. (little)

Cooking instructions:
Heat olive oil in pan. Steam the pumpkin cut in cubes, season with cilantro, pepper and curry, simmer with a little water, salt with sea salt, add chopped parsley with cardamom and turmeric, simmer on a small fire for about 10 minutes, depending on the pumpkin, the pumpkin should still be firm.

Place the rice in salted water, bring to the boil and let it simmer over low heat for about 15 minutes.

9.47 Pumpkin soup

Promotes digestion, forcing spleen and stomach, reduces blood pressure, strengthens immune system, prevents cancer, reduces radiation damage, improves digestion, regenerates skin, lowers cholesterol, reduces blood glucose, protects liver.
Cooking time approx. 1 hour
3 portions to 236,33g. / 105kcal. - (carb:71% / prot:29%)
100g.=44,29kcal. / protein 2,54g. fat:3,64g.
µg. - Ph:4,02 Na:0,96 Ka:24,72 Mg:1,82 Ca:2,89 Fe:0,08 Zn:0,02 Col.:0 Hsr.:1,08

Quantity of ingredients:
Pumpkin 3/4 lbs / 300g. (yes)
Carrot 2 pieces / 100g. (yes)
Potato 2 pieces / 120g. (little)
Olive oil 1 table spoon / 10g. (yes)
Onion white 1 piece / 50g. (yes)
Water 1 cup / 120g. (yes)
Parsley 1 table spoon / 7g. (yes)
Anise (Common Fennel) 1 pinch / 1g. (yes)
Salt 1 pinch / 1g. (little)

Cooking instructions:
Add the olive oil to the pan, add the diced pumpkin, diced carrots and potatoes. Roast them shortly, add the finely chopped onion, fill with water, add enough water to cover the vegetables at least 3 finger-widths. Boil at low heat.

Season with sea salt, add small cutted parsley, a pinch of anise (little). Allow to simmer for about 35 minutes. Then purée the soup and add some water, depending on the consistency of the soup.

9.48 Quick zucchini soup

Diuretic, supports urination. Strengthens gastrointestinal function, expands blood vessels, prevents cancer, prevents diseases (in the elderly). Stimulates liver function, detoxifying.
Cooking time approx. 10 min
4 portions to 241,5g. / 42kcal. - (carb:46% / prot:54%)
100g.=17,29kcal. / protein 1,76g. fat:2,04g.
µg. - Ph:3,81 Na:0,41 Ka:29,78 Mg:3,2 Ca:5,37 Fe:0,21 Zn:0,01 Col.:0 Hsr.:2,85

Quantity of ingredients:
Zucchini 2-3 pieces / 500g. (yes)
Onion white 1 piece / 50g. (yes)
Corn germ oil 2 table spoons / 6g. (yes)
Parsley 1 table spoon / 7g. (yes)
Chives 1 teaspoon / 3g. (yes)
Water 2 cup / 400g. (yes)

Cooking instructions:
Fry chopped onion in oil. Add sliced zucchini and sauté well. Pour with water. Chop parsley and chives, add and puree everything.

9.49 Radish with sugar

Promotes digestion, detoxifying, improves blood circulation, supports urination, reduces thirst, prevents cancer, strengthens body cells, dissolves stagnation, relieves weakness, promotes spleen, calms stomach, strengthens lung.
Cooking time approx. 5 min
2 portions to 202g. / 46kcal. - (carb:71% / prot:29%)
100g.=22,77kcal. / protein 2g. fat:0,4g.
µg. - Ph:7,18 Na:4,46 Ka:79,71 Mg:3,71 Ca:8,17 Fe:0,2 Zn:0,07 Col.:0 Hsr.:2,48

Quantity of ingredients:
Radish (white, green, purple-red) 1 piece / 400g. (yes)
Sugar brown 1 teaspoon / 4g. (yes)

Cooking instructions:
Grate the radish and sprinkle with sugar.

9.50 Refreshing cucumber soup with potatoes

Diuretic, detoxifying, suppresses conversion of sugar into fat, lowers cholesterol, prevents cancer, reduces inflammation, improves digestion, lowers cholesterol, dissolves stagnation, improves blood circulation, stimulates appetite.
Cooking time approx. 15 min
Allergens: GN
3 portions to 307,33g. / 148kcal. - (carb:70% / prot:30%)
100g.=48,26kcal. / protein 3,93g. fat:5,09g.
µg. - Ph:3,72 Na:0,77 Ka:23,54 Mg:1,43 Ca:2 Fe:0,05 Zn:0,02 Col.:0 Hsr.:1,19

Quantity of ingredients:
Sesame oil 1 table spoon / 10g. (little)
Potato 4 pieces / 300g. (little)
Onion (spring onion) 3 pieces / 60g. (yes)
Pepper (ground) 1 pinch / 0,5g. ()
Nutmeg 1 pinch / 1g. (yes)
Salt 1 pinch / 1g. (little)
Lemon 1/2 piece / 25g. (yes)
Cucumber 2 pieces / 500g. (yes)
Cream, sweet 30% 1 table spoon / 10g. (little)
Dill 1 table spoon / 15g. (yes)

Cooking instructions:
Sauté sesame oil, chopped potatoes, plenty of spring onions in a hot pot; add pepper, a little nutmeg, salt, lemon juice, hot water, diced cucumber; simmer for about 10 minutes and then puree; add some sweet cream as you like,
and fresh dill.

Variation: Add a little chili, oregano, thyme or rosemary to soften the cooling effect.

9.51 Rice congee with carrots and fennel

Worms, forcing spleen, relieves constipation, stimulates nerves, detoxifying, reduces inflammation, improves blood circulation, reduces blood pressure, strengthens immune system, prevents cancer, reduces radiation damage.
Cooking time approx. 2 hours and more
Allergens: G
3 portions to 284,67g. / 131kcal. - (carb:94% / prot:6%)
100g.=46,14kcal. / protein 4,17g. fat:1,37g.
µg. - Ph:3,26 Na:3,23 Ka:18,37 Mg:21,62 Ca:22,98 Fe:0,13 Zn:0,03 Col.:0,09 Hsr.:1,26

Quantity of ingredients:
Basic recipe for a rice soup (Congee) 2 cup / 500g. (little)
Carrot 2 pieces / 100g. (yes)
Fennel 1 piece / 250g. (yes)
Butter organic 1 teaspoon / 3g. (yes)
Cardamom 1/2 teaspoon / 1g. (little)

Cooking instructions:
Cook rice congee according to basic recipe.
Clean and cut carrots and fennel.

When carrots and fennel are cooked from the beginning, they serve wholesomeness. If added shortly before the end of the cooking time, taste and vitamins are retained.

Refine with butter and cardamom before serving.

9.52 Rice congee with chicken liver and buckthorn fruit

Good to fight blood circulation disorders, thrombose, risk of embolism, high blood pressure, a headache, heart attack and stroke. Has many vitamins and minerals, high quality amino acid profile. Regulates the blood pressure and blood glucose level, forcing spleen.
Cooking time approx. 3 hours
Allergens: EO
3 portions to 307,67g. / 176kcal. - (carb:94% / prot:6%)
100g.=57,1kcal. / protein 7,51g. fat:1,45g.
µg. - Ph:4,49 Na:2,71 Ka:4,23 Mg:29,58 Ca:28,04 Fe:0,08 Zn:0,05 Col.:1,44 Hsr.:2,41

Quantity of ingredients:
Basic recipe for a rice soup (Congee) 5 cups / 800g. (little)
Chicken liver 1/2 cup / 60g. (little)
Bocksdorn fruits (Fructus Lycii, goji berry dried 1/2 cup / 60g. (little)
Soy sauce 1 dash / 3g. (little)

Cooking instructions:
Cook basic recipe for rice congee with the chicken liver and wolfberry fruits; Season with soy sauce.

9.53 Rice pesto with pine nuts

Worming spleen and stomach, harmonizes the intestine.
Cooking time approx. 30 min
4 portions to 305,75g. / 274kcal. - (carb:71% / prot:29%)
100g.=89,78kcal. / protein 5,71g. fat:10,1g.
µg. - Ph:2,09 Na:0,13 Ka:2,41 Mg:1,09 Ca:0,55 Fe:0,02 Zn:0,02 Col.:0 Hsr.:1,33

Quantity of ingredients:
Rice variety any 1 1/2 cups / 200g. (yes)
Water 4 cup / 950g. (yes)
Garlic 4 big cloves / 8g. (yes)
Basil 1 handful / 15g. (yes)
Pine nuts 3 table spoons / 30g. (little)
Olive oil 2 table spoons / 20g. (yes)

Cooking instructions:
Boil the rice with 1 liter of water. Finely crush the peeled garlic in a
mortar or puree with a hand mixer. Add finely crushed basil leaves, then
purée the pine nuts a little coarser. Lastly, gradually add the oil until a
thick paste forms. Mix the pesto sauce with the finished rice.

9.54 Rice porridge with shallots

Strengths spleen and stomach, strengthens the muscles. Strengthens
gastrointestinal function, expands blood vessels, prevents cancer,
prevents diseases (in the elderly).
Cooking time approx. 25 min
2 portions to 256g. / 177kcal. - (carb:90% / prot:10%)
100g.=69,14kcal. / protein 3,79g. fat:0,61g.
µg. - Ph:6,11 Na:0,54 Ka:5,82 Mg:3,38 Ca:1,45 Fe:0,03 Zn:0,04 Col.:0 Hsr.:6,44

Quantity of ingredients:
Rice variety any 1 cup / 100g. (yes)
Water 4 cups / 400g. (yes)
Onion (spring onion) 2 table spoons / 12g. (yes)

Cooking instructions:
Boil the rice with the water until a porridge is formed. Finely chop onion
and keep for 5 min. to let go.

9.55 Rice with parsnips

Rich in vitamins, minerals potassium and zinc. Good to fight blood
circulation disorders, thrombose, risk of embolism, high blood pressure,
a headache, heart attack and stroke, yeast infections.
Cooking time approx. 45 min
3 portions to 261,33g. / 206kcal. - (carb:78% / prot:22%)
100g.=78,95kcal. / protein 5,16g. fat:4,52g.
µg. - Ph:6,72 Na:0,7 Ka:31,66 Mg:2,54 Ca:3,53 Fe:0,05 Zn:0,07 Col.:0 Hsr.:4,06

Quantity of ingredients:
Rice variety any 1 cup / 120g. (yes)
Water 1 1/2 cups / 200g. (yes)
Salt 1 pinch / 1g. (little)
Parsnip 3-4 pieces / 450g. (yes)
Olive oil 1 table spoon / 10g. (yes)
Sage 1 teaspoon / 3g. (yes)

Cooking instructions:
Peel the parsnips and cut into slices. Fry for a short time in oil. Add the rice and fry again for a short time. Add the water and cook it at least 30 min. Sprinkle with fresh chopped sage.

9.56 Rice with stewed vegetables

Reduces blood pressure, strengthens immune system, prevents cancer, reduces radiation damage, extremely low fat content, good to fight blood circulation disorders, thrombose, risk of embolism, a headache, heart attack and stroke. Is diuretic.
Cooking time approx. 20 min
Allergens: L
2 portions to 310,5g. / 166kcal. - (carb:82% / prot:18%)
100g.=53,62kcal. / protein 4,33g. fat:2,25g.
µg. - Ph:8,31 Na:2,83 Ka:26,32 Mg:3,14 Ca:5,9 Fe:0,2 Zn:0,07 Col.:0 Hsr.:6,32

Quantity of ingredients:
Rice variety any 1/2 cup / 60g. (yes)
Water 3 cups / 300g. (yes)
Lemon peel 1 piece / 3g. (yes)
Water 1/2 cup / 0g. (yes)
Carrot 2 pieces / 180g. (yes)
Celery sticks 1/2 piece / 5g. (yes)
Champignon 1/2 cup / 50g. (little)
Cress 2 table spoons / 20g. (yes)
Linseed oil 1 dash / 3g. (yes)

Cooking instructions:
Cook rice according to basic recipe with a piece of lemon peel. Steam chopped carrots, celery and mushrooms until soft. Then sprinkle with cress. Then add a dash of high quality cold oil.

9.57 Roasted millet with plum compote

Supports urination, promotes spleen and kidney, strengthens the defense. Good to fight fungi infections.
Cooking time approx. 30 min
4 portions to 218,25g. / 139kcal. - (carb:85% / prot:15%)
100g.=63,8kcal. / protein 3,57g. fat:1,24g.
µg. - Ph:2,99 Na:0,1 Ka:4,37 Mg:1,68 Ca:0,78 Fe:0,09 Zn:0,03 Col.:0 Hsr.:0,93

Quantity of ingredients:
Millet 1 cup / 120g. (yes)
Water 1 1/2 cups / 250g. (yes)
Plum 1 1/2 cups / 250g. (little)
Vanilla pod 1 pinch / 1g. (yes)
Water 5/8 lbs - 8oz / 250g. (yes)
Cinnamon ground 1 pinch / 1g. (little)
Acerola fruit nectar or powder 1/2 teaspoon / 1g. (little)

Cooking instructions:
Roast millet briefly, pour over water, heat till it boils and let stand for 20 min. to swell.
Cook plums with water, vanilla and cinnamon 10 min. then strain. Add acerola and add to the millet.

9.58 Rosemary Potatoes

Reduces Inflammation, improves digestion, regenerates skin, supports urination, lowers cholesterol. Rosemary stimulates digestion, strengthens lung, promotes spleen and kidney, dries out.
Cooking time approx. 30 min
2 portions to 216,5g. / 188kcal. - (carb:76% / prot:24%)
100g.=87,07kcal. / protein 4,21g. fat:5,25g.
µg. - Ph:11,51 Na:0,72 Ka:82,88 Mg:4,72 Ca:1,86 Fe:0,1 Zn:0,07 Col.:0 Hsr.:3,64

Quantity of ingredients:
Potato 6-8 pieces / 420g. (little)
Salt (herbal) 1 pinch / 1g. (little)
Olive oil 1 table spoon / 10g. (yes)
Rosemary 1 teaspoon / 2g. (yes)

Cooking instructions:
Cut the potatoes into half´s, apply a little olive oil on the cut surface, then salt, sprinkle 2 - 3 rosemary needles on the potatoes.
Place the potatoes on the baking tray and bake them in the preheated oven for approx. 25 minutes to 190°C/374°F.

9.59 Semolina soup with vegetables

Reduces blood pressure, strengthens immune system, prevents cancer, forcing spleen, dissolves stagnation, promotes weight loss. Good to fight immunodeficiency, loss of appetite, flatulence, high blood pressure, depressions, diabetes, diarrhea, rheumatism, heartburn, twelffinger intestinal ulcers.
Cooking time approx. 20 min
Allergens: AGL
3 portions to 237,67g. / 105kcal. - (carb:85% / prot:15%)
100g.=44,32kcal. / protein 2,38g. fat:4,24g.
µg. - Ph:2,88 Na:3,04 Ka:8,54 Mg:9,5 Ca:37,49 Fe:0,11 Zn:0,03 Col.:0 Hsr.:1,7

Quantity of ingredients:
Basic recipe for a vegetable soup (nutritious) 2 cup / 500g. (little)
Wheat semolina 2 table spoons / 20g. (yes)
Lovage 1/2 teaspoon / 2g. (yes)
Basil (fresh) 1/2 teaspoon / 1g. (yes)
Nutmeg 1 pinch / 0,1g. (yes)
Carrot 1/4 lbs - 4oz / 100g. (yes)
Celery root 1/8 lbs - 2oz / 50g. (yes)
Cream, sweet 30% 3 table spoons / 30g. (little)
Parsley 1 table spoon / 10g. (yes)

Cooking instructions:
Roast wheat grits without fat in a pan. Roast the chopped carrots and celery briefly. Add the vegetable soup (Basic recipe for a vegetable soup). Season with lovage, nutmeg and let it 10 min. simmer.
Stir in the cream before serving and garnish with parsley.

9.60 Spicy Tofu Vegetable Pan

Forcing spleen, relieves constipation, detoxifying, reduces inflammation, improves blood circulation, promotes sweating, dissolves stagnation, reduces flatulence, reduces blood pressure, strengthens immune system, prevents cancer, reduces radiation damage.
Cooking time approx. 25 min
Allergens: EN
4 portions to 329,25g. / 241kcal. - (carb:67% / prot:33%)
100g.=73,27kcal. / protein 7,37g. fat:7,32g.
µg. - Ph:3,76 Na:4,32 Ka:9,86 Mg:2,38 Ca:3,32 Fe:0,08 Zn:0,02 Col.:0,01 Hsr.:1,82

Quantity of ingredients:
Sesame oil 2 table spoons / 20g. (little)
Carrot 2 pieces / 100g. (yes)
Fennel 1 piece / 250g. (yes)
Leek 1 piece / 200g. (yes)
Salt 1 pinch / 1g. (little)
Turmeric (yellow root) 1 pinch / 1g. (little)
Lemon juice 1 splash / 1g. (yes)
Soy Tofu 1 package / 120g. (little)
Pepper (ground) 1 pinch / 0,5g. ()
Soy sauce 1 dash / 3g. (little)
Rice (whole grain) 1 cup / 120g. (yes)
Water 6 cups / 500g. (yes)
Salt 1 pinch / 1g. (little)

Cooking instructions:
Heat sesame oil in a hot wok or a hot pan; fry the chopped carrots, fennel and leek slices; salt, a dash of lemon juice, turmeric, tofu cubes roast for 1 - 2 minutes.
Add the pepper and cook covered for about 5 minutes; drizzle with soy sauce.
Place the rice in salted water, heat till it boils and let it simmer over low heat for about 15 minutes.

9.61 Tea from juniper berry

Promotes digestion, diuretic, dries out, good to fight loss of appetite, diarrhea, dehydrates, gastrointestinal complaints, muscle rheumatism and pyelonephritis, heartburn, germicidal, improves blood circulation.
Cooking time approx. 10 min
1 portion to 128g. / 10kcal. - (carb:52% / prot:48%)
100g.=7,81kcal. / protein 0,55g. fat:0,44g.
µg. - Ph:11,84 Na:1,4 Ka:30,07 Mg:6,65 Ca:28,72 Fe:0,05 Zn:0,11 Col.:0 Hsr.:0

Quantity of ingredients:
Juniper berry 1 teaspoon / 3g. (yes)
Water 1 cup / 125g. (yes)

Cooking instructions:
A teaspoon of dried juniper berries for a cup of tea. Start cold and bring to the boil. Let it sit for 15 minutes, then strain.
This tea is unsweetened and swallowed, slowly drunk. The amount is enough for one day.

9.62 Tea Green tea

Green tea promotes digestion, supports urination, dissolves mucus, detoxifying, stimulates nerves, reduces blood lipids, lowers cholesterol, reduces inflammation.
Cooking time approx. 10 min
1 portion to 122g. / 2kcal. - (carb:20% / prot:80%)
100g.=1,64kcal. / protein 0g. fat:0g.
µg. - Ph:5,61 Na:1,07 Ka:27,59 Mg:4,07 Ca:9,43 Fe:0,03 Zn:0,1 Col.:0 Hsr.:0

Quantity of ingredients:
Green tea 1 teaspoon / 2g. (yes)
Water 1 cup / 120g. (yes)

Cooking instructions:
For each cup you use a teaspoonful or a teabag.
Pour green tea only with 60 to 80 ° C / 140 to 176 °F hot water, otherwise it will be bitter.
If the tea has a stimulating effect, let it draw for two to three minutes. It has a calming effect for a duration of five minutes (no longer, otherwise it will be bitter!).
Another method: Pour the tea leaves with about 70 ° C / 158 °F hot water and pour the water immediately again. Then just pour hot water again. The bitter substances disappear and the tea gets a milder aroma.

9.63 Thick pea soup

Supports urination, detoxifying, dissolves stagnation, improves blood circulation, strengthens liver and kidney, strengthens immune system.
Cooking time approx. 2-3 hours
Allergens: AN
3 portions to 255g. / 123kcal. - (carb:47% / prot:53%)
100g.=48,37kcal. / protein 4,36g. fat:7,3g.
µg. - Ph:3,44 Na:0,25 Ka:7,5 Mg:1,22 Ca:1,55 Fe:0,06 Zn:0,04 Col.:0 Hsr.:5,21

Quantity of ingredients:
Peas, green 3/8 lbs - 6oz / 150g. (little)
Water 2 1/4 cups / 550g. (yes)
Sesame oil 1 table spoon / 20g. (little)
Onion white 1/2 piece / 25g. (yes)
Ginger fresh 1/2 teaspoon / 1g. (yes)
Ground 1/2 teaspoon / 1g. (yes)
Oat meal 1 table spoon / 15g. (yes)
Salt 1 pinch / 1g. (little)

Cooking instructions:
Soak dried peas before cooking. Sauté sesame oil, onion, a little oatmeal, ginger and cumin in a hot pot; add the peas and simmer for 2-3 hours; add salt at the end and purée with a blender; garnish with parsley.

9.64 Tomato soup

Promotes digestion, helps to digest fat, supports urination, reduces blood pressure, dissolves stagnation. Contains unsaturated fatty acids, is antioxidative.
Cooking time approx. 10 min
2 portions to 290g. / 100kcal. - (carb:42% / prot:58%)
100g.=34,66kcal. / protein 1,78g. fat:7,9g.
µg. - Ph:4,2 Na:1,2 Ka:31,36 Mg:1,99 Ca:3,85 Fe:0,07 Zn:0,04 Col.:0,01 Hsr.:1,47

Quantity of ingredients:
Olive oil 1 table spoon / 15g. (yes)
Onion white 1 piece / 60g. (yes)
Cinnamon ground 1 pinch / 1g. (little)
Basil (fresh) 1 teaspoon / 2g. (yes)
Pepper (ground) 1 pinch / 0,5g. ()
Salt 1 pinch / 1g. (little)
Tomato 6 pieces / 250g. (yes)
Water 5/8 lbs - 8oz / 250g. (yes)
Peppers powder 1 pinch / 1g. (little)

Cooking instructions:
Roast the onion in a pot. Salt and spices. Briefly roast. Put washed and quartered tomatoes in the pan. Stir and sauté briefly. Add a quart of water and heat till it boils. Cook for a quarter of an hour and puree.

9.65 Vegetable bowl with tofu and curry on rice

Diuretic, reduces blood glucose. Reduces flatulence, supports digestion. Contains ideal herbal mucus, which provides regeneration of the small and large intestinal flora. Reduces blood pressure, strengthens immune system.
Cooking time approx. 30 min
Allergens: E
6 portions to 400,17g. / 162kcal. - (carb:56% / prot:44%)
100g.=40,48kcal. / protein 8,62g. fat:6,02g.
µg. - Ph:1,42 Na:0,6 Ka:6,19 Mg:0,81 Ca:1,42 Fe:0,02 Zn:0,01 Col.:0 Hsr.:0,6

Quantity of ingredients:
Olive oil 2 table spoons / 20g. (yes)
Garlic 2 cloves / 3g. (yes)
Onion white 1 piece / 60g. (yes)
Curry 2 table spoons / 16g. (yes)
Water 2 cup / 500g. (yes)
Turnips 2 pieces / 50g. (little)
Pumpkin 1 piece / 400g. (yes)
Carrot 1 piece / 100g. (yes)
Parsnip 1 piece / 150g. (yes)
Potato 1 piece / 70g. (little)
Sweet potato 1 piece / 70g. (little)
Cauliflower 1/4 piece / 250g. (yes)
Broccoli 1/2 piece / 250g. (little)
Okra 12 pieces / 200g. (little)
Soy Tofu 1 piece / 250g. (little)
Basil 3 table spoons / 12g. (yes)
Salt 1 pinch / 0,5g. (little)

Cooking instructions:
Heat the oil at medium temperature in a large, heavy casserole, add the garlic and onion and sauté with constant stirring. Sprinkle curry powder over it, fry gently for about 5 minutes and make sure that the garlic and curry do not burn. Add the water and heat till it boils. Gradually peel all vegetables, dice and add, starting with the varieties that need the longest cooking time. Once the water has boiled again, reduce the heat and simmer the vegetables for about 15 minutes. When it is almost soft. Add the cauliflower and broccoli florets and the okra and cook the stew for another 10 to 15 minutes. Add the tofu during the last 5 minutes. Cook the brown rice at the same time: Sprinkle the rice in a medium saucepan with water, salt and cover for about 20 minutes. cook on a low heat. Take from the fire and another 10 min. to let go.
Arrange the stew over the brown rice and sprinkle with basil.

9.66 Vegetable miso soup with tofu

Very powerful, strengthens after febrile illness, reduces blood pressure, strengthens immune system, prevents cancer, reduces radiation damage, improves blood circulation, strengthens liver and kidney, detoxifying, strengthens the muscles, reduces flatulence, forcing spleen.
Cooking time approx. 15 min
Allergens: EN

4 portions to 247,75g. / 107kcal. - (carb:22% / prot:78%)
100g.=43,09kcal. / protein 1,85g. fat:9,4g.
µg. - Ph:3,92 Na:13,88 Ka:10,98 Mg:1,98 Ca:4,08 Fe:0,07 Zn:0,01 Col.:0 Hsr.:1,45

Quantity of ingredients:
Sesame oil 2 table spoons / 35g. (little)
Onion (shallot) 1 piece / 20g. (yes)
Carrot 1 piece / 70g. (yes)
Leek 2 inches / 10g. (yes)
Water 3 cups / 750g. (yes)
Endive salad 2 table spoons / 30g. (yes)
Soy Tofu 2 table spoons / 30g. (little)
Ginger fresh 1/2 teaspoon / 1g. (yes)
Miso 2 table spoons / 15g. (little)

Cooking instructions:
In sesame oil first sauté onions, then carrots and a little leek; Pour in
water and simmer gently; add the bean sprouts and endive leaves and
leave to stand; Tofu cubes, add a little ginger; at the end stir in a little
cooled cooking-water the Miso.

9.67 Vegetable rice

Forcing spleen, dissolves stagnation. Good to fight immunodeficiency,
loss of appetite, flatulence, high blood pressure, strengthens kidney and
bladder. Diuretic, warming the body from the inside.
internal organs functions.
Cooking time approx. 30 min
Allergens: L
3 portions to 274,67g. / 304kcal. - (carb:88% / prot:12%)
100g.=110,56kcal. / protein 8,1g. fat:3,4g.
µg. - Ph:11,8 Na:1,92 Ka:15,55 Mg:11,36 Ca:27,38 Fe:0,16 Zn:0,07 Col.:0 Hsr:5,17

Quantity of ingredients:
Broccoli 1/8 lbs - 2oz / 50g. (little)
Carrot 1/8 lbs - 2oz / 50g. (yes)
Kohlrabi 1/8 lbs - 2oz / 50g. (little)
Cauliflower 1 oz / 30g. (yes)
Peas 1/2 oz / 20g. (little)
Margarine 1 teaspoon / 4g. (yes)
Rice (whole grain) 5/8 oz / 200g. (yes)
Basic recipe for a vegetable soup (nutritious) 7/8 lbs / 400g. (little)
Parsley 1/2 oz / 20g. (yes)
Pepper (ground) 1 pinch / 0,2g. ()

Cooking instructions:
Cut the broccoli, carrots and kohlrabi into small cubes, divide the cauliflower into small florets. Heat the margarine in a pan or saucepan, sauté the vegetables. Then add the rice, top up with the vegetable stock and leave to soak for 15-20 minutes.

In the meantime, finely chop the parsley. After cooking, season the rice with freshly ground pepper and parsley.

9.68 Vegetable semolina soup

Diuretic, harmonizes the stomach and intestines, conducts bowel winds, reduces blood pressure, lowers cholesterol, detoxifying, good to fight loss of appetite, flatulence, inflammatory bowel disease, heartburn, twelffinger intestinal ulcers. Stimulates digestion, reduces pain.
Cooking time approx. 20 min
Allergens: AEGL
3 portions to 459,67g. / 199kcal. - (carb:79% / prot:21%)
100g.=43,22kcal. / protein 6,38g. fat:7,02g.
µg. - Ph:4,26 Na:4,63 Ka:23,27 Mg:6,33 Ca:22,08 Fe:0,09 Zn:0,04 Col.:0,39 Hsr.:2,88

Quantity of ingredients:
Basic recipe for a vegetable soup (nutritious) 2 cup / 500g. (little)
Potato 1 piece / 80g. (little)
Parsnip 1 piece / 180g. (yes)
Carrot 1 piece / 120g. (yes)
Celery root 3/8 lbs - 6oz / 150g. (yes)
Kohlrabi 1/2 piece / 200g. (little)
Beans (green, fresh) 1/4 lbs / 100g. (little)
Wheat semolina 2 table spoons / 24g. (yes)
Lovage 1/2 teaspoon / 2g. (yes)
Butter organic 1 table spoon / 20g. (yes)
Soy sauce 1 teaspoon / 3g. (little)

Cooking instructions:
Worm the prepared vegetable soup; cook the vegetables in the soup softly. Spread some wheatgrass and let it swell. At the end, add lovage-green and a little butter and taste with soy sauce.

9.69 Warming carrot soup

Strengthens and warms, reduces blood pressure, strengthens immune system, prevents cancer, reduces radiation damage, strengthens gastrointestinal function.
Cooking time approx. 30 min
Allergens: HL
3 portions to 274,67g. / 133kcal. - (carb:79% / prot:21%)
100g.=48,54kcal. / protein 2,16g. fat:7,86g.
µg. - Ph:2,86 Na:2,31 Ka:9,18 Mg:8,37 Ca:32,64 Fe:0,13 Zn:0,03 Col.:0 Hsr.:1

Quantity of ingredients:
Carrot 4 pieces / 250g. (yes)
Walnut oil 2 table spoons / 20g. (little)
Onion (shallot) 2 pieces / 40g. (yes)
Anise (Common Fennel) 1/2 teaspoon / 1g. (yes)
Nutmeg 1 pinch / 1g. (yes)
Ginger fresh 1/2 teaspoon / 1g. (yes)
Salt 1 pinch / 1g. (little)
Basic recipe for a vegetable soup (nutritious) 2 cup / 500g. (little)
Parsley 1 table spoon / 10g. (yes)

Cooking instructions:
Heat walnut oil in a hot pot and fry onions; steam the carrots in it; add anise, nutmeg, a little ginger, salt and sauté everything; add water or vegetable- or meat stock; cook everything soft and then puree; fold in parsley at the end.

Recommendation: Suitable for the cold season, especially if you use meat broth as a liquid for infusion.

9.70 Wheat semolina with olives-herb-sauce and salad

Protects the digestive system. Detoxifying, affects anorexia, good to fight flatulence, inflammatory bowel disease, obesity, gout, stomach ulcers, stomach cramps, rheumatism, heartburn. Dissolves stagnation, relieves fatigue.
Cooking time approx. 15 min
Allergens: ACGL
3 portions to 291g. / 245kcal. - (carb:77% / prot:23%)
100g.=84,08kcal. / protein 7,65g. fat:9,46g.
µg. - Ph:4,44 Na:2,51 Ka:6,39 Mg:7,97 Ca:30,53 Fe:0,1 Zn:0,04 Col.:3,02 Hsr.:2,72

Quantity of ingredients:
Cream, sweet 30% 1/8 lbs - 2oz / 40g. (little)
Water 1/3 cup / 65g. (yes)
Wheat semolina 1/4 lbs - 4oz / 100g. (yes)
Chicken egg 1 piece / 60g. (yes)
Pepper (ground) 1 pinch / 0,5g. ()
Lemon peel 1 pinch / 1g. (yes)
Onion white 1 piece / 60g. (yes)
Olive oil 1 teaspoon / 2g. (yes)
Chives 1 table spoon / 7g. (yes)
Basic recipe for a vegetable soup (nutritious) 2 cups / 500g. (little)
Lettuce 2 handful / 30g. (yes)
Olive oil 1 teaspoon / 3g. (yes)
Lemon juice 1 teaspoon / 3g. (yes)
Oregano fresh 1 teaspoon / 2g. (yes)

Cooking instructions:
Mix cream and water and heat till it boils. Stir in the wheat semolina and cook to a thick porridge and remove from heat. Whisk the egg and stir in, season with pepper and grated lemon zest. Form with 2 coffee spoons, dumplings and leave to stir in the slightly boiling vegetable stock until the dumplings float up.
Chop the onion and roast it in olive oil in a pan. Pour the semolina dumplings into the pan and sprinkle with finely chopped chives.

Wash salad and cut into thin strips. Season with olive oil, lemon juice and oregano.

9.71 Zucchini semolina cream soup

Good to fight loss of appetite, reduces blood pressure, promotes weight loss. Good to fight loss of appetite, flatulence, inflammatory bowel disease, rheumatism, heartburn.
Cooking time approx. 25 min
Allergens: AGL
4 portions to 341,75g. / 146kcal. - (carb:78% / prot:22%)
100g.=42,72kcal. / protein 4,02g. fat:7,8g.
μg. - Ph:1,7 Na:0,83 Ka:9,09 Mg:4,88 Ca:18,35 Fe:0,08 Zn:0,02 Col.:0,22 Hsr.:0,82

Quantity of ingredients:
Butter organic 1/2 oz / 20g. (yes)
Wheat semolina 2 table spoons / 20g. (yes)
Parsley 1 Bunch / 100g. (yes)
Basic recipe for a vegetable soup (nutritious) 3 1/2 cups / 800g. (little)

Lovage 1/2 teaspoon / 2g. (yes)
Nutmeg 1 pinch / 0,5g. (yes)
Anise (Common Fennel) 1 pinch / 0,5g. (yes)
Zucchini 7/8 lbs / 400g. (yes)
Ginger fresh 1/2 teaspoon / 1g. (yes)
Crème fraiche cheese 2 table spoons / 20g. (little)
Lemon peel 1/4 piece / 2g. (yes)
Salt 1 pinch / 1g. (little)
Pepper (ground) 1 pinch / 0,5g. ()

Cooking instructions:
Melt the butter in a saucepan, add the semolina and fry briefly while stirring. Add half of the chopped parsley, sauté for a short time, pour vegetable broth according to the basic recipe, season with chopped lovage, nutmeg and anise. Cook the soup without lid lightly for 10 minutes. Add the finely chopped zucchini and the small piece of lemon zest, cook gently for 5 minutes until the zucchini are tender. Remove the lemon peel.
Using the blender, finely puree the soup with the crème fraiche and the remaining parsley.

10 Effects of food

10.1 Use ingredients: recommendable

Acai powder
Bitter Herb liqueur
Cream 10% coffee cream
Fox nut, gorgon nut, makhana
Fresh cheese from soya
Hibiscus

Kudzu
Lily bulbs
Mascarpone cheese
Noodles (wheat) with egg
Noodles (whole grain) with egg

10.2 Use ingredients: yes

Adzuki beans
Agar agar (kelp)
Agave nectar
Angelica root
Anise (Common Fennel)
Arrowroot
Asparagus (green or white)
Aubergine
Avocado
Balm
Bamboo shoots
Banchatee (green tea)
barberry
Barley
Barley flour
Barley grass powder
Barley grouts
Barley malt
Barley not peeled
Basil
Basil (fresh)
Batavia
Bay leaf
Bearberry leaf
Bitter Lemon
Bitter orange peel
Black caraway
Blackberry leaves
Blue mallow tee
Borage
Borage oil
Boxhorn clover seeds
Bread roll
Bread with carob kernel flour
Breadcrumbs (wheat bread, bread roll)
Buckbean
Buckwheat
Buckwheat (roasted) Kasha
Buckwheat whole grain
Bulgur (cereals)

Burdock root tea
Butter (half fat)
Butter organic
Capers in olive oil
Carob flour, St. john's bread
Carrot
Carrot (Early Carrot)
Carrot juice without sugar
Cauliflower
Celery root
Celery sticks
Cereal coffee
Chamomile
Chamomile tea
Chervil
Chervil dried
Chicken egg
Chicken egg white
Chicken meat
Chicken yolk
Chicory
Chili (pod or ground)
Chives
Chlorella (fresh water)
Chrysanthemum blossom tea
Cinnamon sticks
Clarified butter
Clove
Coconut flakes
Coconut grated
Coconut meat
Coconut milk
Cooking oil
Coriander
Coriander (fresh)
Corn
Corn (fast polenta)
Corn (roasted)
Corn flour
Corn germ oil

Corn Grease (Polenta)
Corn silk tea
Corn starch
Couscous
Cream sour 10%
Creamer
Cress
Crispbread
Cucumber
Cucumber (bitter)
Cucumber (spicy cucumber)
Cumin (Caraway seed)
Curcuma
Curry
Curry paste red
Daisy
Dandelion (young plants)
Dandelion juice
Dandelionroots tea
Dashi
Dates dried
Dates red
Dill
Dyer's broom herb
Eel
Elderberry blossom tee
Endive salad
Evening primrose oil
Fennel
Fennel seeds ground
Fennel tea
Fenugreek (Trigonella foenum-
graecum)
Flounder
Flower pollen
Fresh cheese with herbs
Fructose (glucose)
Garam Masala powder
Garlic
Gelee Royal
Gentian root
Gentian root tea
Ginger fresh
Ginger oil
Ginger powder
Ginseng
Ginseng root
Gourd
Grapefruit (Pomelo)
Grapefruit dried peel
Grapefruit juice
Grapes red
Grapes white
Grapeseed oil

Green tea
Ground
Ground caraway
Hawthorn
Herbal tea mix
Herbs bitter
Herbs of Provence
Herbs various
Herbs wild
Hibiscus tea
Hokkaido pumpkin
Honey
Horehound leaves
Hyssop
Iceberg lettuce
Jasmine blossoms tee
Juniper berry
King Solomon's-seal
Kukicha tea
Kumquats
Lamb's lettuce
Lavender blossoms
Leaf salads (bitter)
Leek
Lemon
Lemon Balm (dried)
Lemon Balm (fresh)
Lemon juice
Lemon peel
Lemongrass
Lettuce
Lime
Lime blossom tea
Linseed oil
Liver smoothing tea
Lotus roots
Lotus seeds
Lovage
Lovage seeds
Luo Han Guo fruit
Lye roll
Mallow (Malva sylvestris) blossom tea
Malt
Maple syrup
Margarine
Marjoram
Millet
Millet flakes
Mineral water
Mulled Wine Spice
Multi-grain bread (gray bread)
Nasturtium (nose-twister or nose-
tweaker)
Nettles

Nori, purple seaweed, red algae
Nutmeg
Oat
Oat flakes (whole grain)
Oat flakes roasted
Oat flour
Oat fusion (baby food)
Oat meal
Olive oil
Olives
Olives green
Onion (shallot)
Onion (spring onion)
Onion read
Onion white
Oregano dried
Oregano fresh
Palm oil
Parsley
Parsley root
Parsnip
Passion blossoms tea
Pearl barley
Pearl barley
Pepper (ground)
Pepper Cayenne
Pepper white (ground)
Peppercorns
Peppermint
Peppermint tea
Pepperoni
Pepperoni, red, pitted, halved
Pepperoni, yellow, pitted, halved
Peppers
Peppers (rose peppers)
Peppers (sweet)
Pickle
Psyllium seed
Pudding powder vanilla
Puff pastry
Pumpkin
Pumpkin seed oil
Radicchio
Radish
Radish (white, green, purple-red)
Radish black
Radish horseradish
Radish leaves
Rapeseed oil
Raspberry leaf tea
Red beet
Red berry (without sugar)
Ribworttea
Rice (fragrance)

Rice (Gaoliang / Sorghum)
Rice (whole grain)
Rice Basmati
Rice black
Rice flour
Rice long grain rice
Rice malt
Rice mash
Rice noodles
Rice red
Rice round grain
Rice starch
Rice sticky
Rice sweet
Rice variety any
Rice wild (nature rice)
Rose blossom tea
Rose leaf tea
Rosemary
Rusk
Rye
Rye flour
Safflower (Dyer's thistle / Hong Hua)
Sage
Sago (cereals)
Salsify
Sourdough
Spelled flakes
Spelled grain
Spelled semolina
Spurdog (spiny dogfish, Schillerlocken)
St. Benedict's thistle, blessed thistle,
holy thistle, spotted thistle
Strawberry jam
Sugar - icing sugar
Sugar brown
Sugar candy white
Sugar cane sugar
Sugar fructose - fruit sugar
Sugar glucose - grapes sugar
Sugar Milk Sugar
Sugar molasses
Sugar palm sugar
Sugar substitute (sweetener)
Sugar white
Tarragon (Estragon)
Tea mixture uric acid lowering
Thistle oil
Thyme
Thyme dried
Tomato
Tomato puree
Valerian
Vanilla

Vanilla pod
Vanilla powder
Vanilla sugar natural
Vinegar (Apple vinegar)
Vinegar (Red wine vinegar)
Vinegar Aceto Balsamico
Vinegar Aceto Balsamico white
Water
Water hot
Watermelon
Wax gourd
Wheat
Wheat bulgur
Wheat flakes
Wheat flatbread/pita bread
Wheat flour
Wheat germ oil
Wheat semolina
Wheat semolina for children
Wheatgrass juice
Wheatgrass powder
White bread (baguette)
White bread (pretzel sticks)
White bread (roll)
White bread (wheat bread)
White breadcrumbs
White dumpling bread (wheat bread cut into chunks)
Wild garlic (garlic spinach)
Wild herbs
Wild strawberries
Wormwood herb
Yam root, yam root tuber
Yarrow
Yarrow tea
Yoghurt vanilla
Yogi tea
Yogurt (natural, 1.5% fat)
Yogurt (natural, 3.5% fat)
Zucchini

10.3 Use ingredients: little

Acerola fruit nectar or powder
Agrimony
Aloe juice
Amaranth
Amaranth Pops
Anchovy / Sardine
Apple (sour)
Apple (sweet)
Apple puree
Apricot
Apricot jam
Apricots
Artichoke
Baking powder
Basic recipe for a beef soup
Basic recipe for a beef soup (warming)
Basic recipe for a chicken soup (warming)
Basic recipe for a duck soup
Basic recipe for a fish soup
Basic recipe for a rice soup (Congee)
Basic recipe for a vegetable soup (nutritious)
Bean oil
Beans (green, fresh)
Beef bone marrow
Beef fillet
Beef heart
Beef heart (calf)
Beef kidney
Beef liver
Beef lungs (calf)
Beef meat
Beef meat (calf)
Beef meatbones
Beef Oxtail pieces
Beef soup meat
Beef stomach
Berries of the season
Bitter liqueur
Black beans
Black fungus mushroom
Black tea
Blackberry dried (unripe fruit)
Blackberry jam
Blackberry´s
Black-eyed peas
Blackthorn (Sloe)
Blueberry
Blueberry dried
Blueberry jam
Bocksdorn fruits (Fructus Lycii, Goji, goji berry dried
Brazil nuts
Brie cheese
Broad beans (thick beans)
Broccoli
Brown ale
Brussels sprouts
Bush beans

Butter beans white
Buttermilk
Calamari
Camembert
Campari
Cantaloupe
Carambola (Star fruit)
Cardamom
Carp
Cashews
Caviar
Champignon
Channa-Dal
Chenpi (chinese tangerine bowl)
Cherry
Cherry (sour)
Cherry compote
Chestnut puree
Chestnuts
Chicken Blood
Chicken heart
Chicken liver
Chicken stomach
Chickpeas
Chickweed
Chinese cabbage
Chinese pearl barley
Cinnamon ground
Clementine
Clementines
Cocoa
Coconut fat
Cod
Codfish
Coffee
Coix (seeds) YiYi Ren
Compote (fruits of the season)
Cottage cheese
Cow's milk (1.5% fat)
Cow's milk (whole milk 3.5% fat)
Crab
Cranberries
Cranberry
Cranberry
Cranberry jam
Cranberry juice
Cream (30% fat)
Cream sour 20%
Cream sour 30%
Cream, sweet 30%
Créme fraiche cheese
Crucian
Curd cheese 20%
Curd cheese 40%

Currant (black)
Currant (red)
Currant (white)
Currant jam (black)
Currant jam (red)
Deer meat
Deer meat
Deer's Bones
Deer's kidneys
Duck (heart)
Duck (slaughtered)
Ducks egg
Dulse (seaweed)
Edam cheese
Eel smoked
Elderberries
Fernet Branca (herbal bitter liqueur)
Feta cheese
Feta cheese
Fig
Fish innards
Fish pieces mixed (fresh water)
Fish remains
Fish sauce
French beans
Fresh cheese
Freshwater crab
Freshwater fish
Gail plum
Galangal
Gelatin white
Ginkgo fruit
Ginseng liqueur
Goat
Goat and sheep's blood
Goat and sheep's brain
Goat and sheep's liver
Goat and sheep's milk
Goat and sheep's stomach
Goat cheese
Goose
Goose blood
Goose egg
Goose fat
Goose parts
Gooseberry
Gorgonzola
Gouda cheese
Grape juice red
Grape juice white
Grass carp
Green spelt
Greengage
Guava

Halibut (Flatfish)
Herring
Hijiki
Honey wine (Met)
Hop
Horse meat
Jellyfish
Kaki plum
Kalmus
Kefir
Kidney beans (red)
Kiwi
Kohlrabi
Kombu seaweed (Saccharina japonica)
Ladyfingers
Lamb bones
Lamb kidneys
Lamb liver
Lamb meat
Lamb shoulder
Lamb's lettuce
Lentils
Lentils black
Lentils red
Lentils yellow
Licorice root tea
Lima beans
Linseed
Linseed (crushed)
Lobster
Longane
Loquate / Japanese medlar
Lychee
Lychee in Preserved
Lychee liqueur
Mackerel
Mango
Mango juice
Manioc flour
Mare's milk
Margarine (diet)
Martini
Mayonnaise 50%
Mayonnaise 80%
Mediterranean fish (cod, plaice,
haddock, sea eel, mackerel)
Medlar
Mirabelle plum
Miso
Miso black (fermented)
Miso paste (soy bean paste)
Mixed Pickles
Mold cheese
Morel (black, dried)

Morel, dried
Mozzarella
Mu Erh Mushroom
Muesli
Mulberry fruit
Mullet
Mung bean
Mung bean sprouting
Mussels
Mustard
Mustard Dijon
Mustard medium hot
Mustard seeds
Mustard sweet
Mutton
Mutton
Nectarine
Oat milk
Octopus
Octopus
Okra
Orange
Orange blossom
Orange dried peel
Orange grated peel
Orange jam
Orange peel
Oyster shell powder
Papaya
Passion fruit
Peaches
Peaches (canned)
Peanut (roasted)
Peanut butter
Peanut oil
Peanuts
Pear
Peas
Peas, green
Pepper powder (hot)
Peppers powder
Perch
Pheasant
Pig blood
Pigeon
Pigeon egg
Pimento
Pine nuts
Pineapple
Pineapple juice without sugar
Pinto beans speckled
Plaice
Plum
Plums

Pomegranate
Pork Bacon
Pork brain
Pork fat (lard)
Pork ham
Pork ham cooked
Pork ham smoked
Pork heart
Pork kidneys
Pork knuckle
Pork Lard
Pork liver
Pork lung
Pork marrow bones
Pork meat
Pork sausage (Bratwurst) Pork skin
Pork stomach
Pork/beef sausage (smoked)
Pork's intestine
Potato
Potato (mealy)
Potato flour
Prickly pear
Prosecco
Pumpernickel (dark bread)
Pumpkin seeds
Quail
Quail egg
Quince
Quinoa
Rabbit
Rabbit (wild)
Rabbit liver
Rabbit meat
Raspberry
Raspberry dried (immature)
Raspberry jam
Red cabbage
Reishi mushroom
Rhubarb
Romaine lettuce / lettuce salad
Rose hip
Rose hip tea
Rosefish
Rucola
Rye wholemeal bread
Saffron
Sake

Salmon
Salt
Salt (herbal)
Sauerkraut (cutted cabbage fermented)
Savory

Savoy cabbage / kale
Sea buckthorn
Sea cucumber
Seacrab
Sesame oil
Sesame oil roasted
Shark
Sheep's milk
Sheep's milk yoghurt
Sherry (whine)
Shrimp
Shrimps
Skim milk powder
Slug
Sorrel
Sour cherries
Sour cream 15% fat
Sour milk
Sour milk cheese 20%
Soy flour
Soy noodles
Soy sauce
Soy Tofu
Soy Tofu smoked
Soya Cuisine (soy cream)
Soybean milk
Soybean oil
Soybeans
Soybeans, black
Soybeans, blacks, fermented
Soybeans, yellow
Spelled (Dark) bread
Spelled wholemeal flour
Spiny lobsters
Spirit
Star anise
Stevia (candyleaf, sweetleaf)
Strawberries
Strawberry Juice
Sunflower oil
Sweet potato
Tabasco
Tangerine
Toast bread (whole grain)
Tomato dried
Tomato juice
Tomato paste
Tonic Water
Topinambur
Trout
Truffle
Tsampa (roasted barley flour)
Tuna
Turkey breast meat

Turkey ham
Turmeric (yellow root)
Turnip
Turnips
Umeboshi paste
Umeboshi plums (Japanese apricots)
Vegetable juice
Wakame
Walnut oil
Wheat beer
Wheat bran
Wheat flour whole grain

Wheat/Rye/Gray-black bread with yeast
Whey
White beans
White cabbage
White wine
Whitefish
Whole grain bread
Wholemeal flour
Wild boar meat
Wormwood
Yeast
Yew nut

10.4 Do not use contra-acting foods

Almond
Almond marzipan
Almond milk
Almond puree
Apple juice (natural cloudy)
Apricot dried
Apricot nectar
Apricots juice
Banana
Banana (cooking banana)
Beer (alcohol-free)
Beer (alcohol-reduced)
Beer (Pils)
Beer (Top-fermented German dark beer)
Berry juice
Blueberry juice
Boletus mushroom
Chanterelle
Chard
Cherry juice
Chocolate
Chocolate (Diabetic)
Cola drink
Cola drink (low calorie)
Currant juice (black)
Currants (black)
Currants (red)
Emmental cheese

Fig dried
Fruit mix juice
Fruit tea
Hazelnuts
Orange juice
Oyster mushroom
Oysters
Parmesan
Pear juice
Pineapple (from a can)
Pistachios
Plum dried
Poppy
Processed cheese 12%
processed cheese 30%
Raisins
Red wine
Rum
Sesame paste (Tahini)
Sesame, black
Sesame, white
Shiitake, dried
Spinach
Sunflower seeds
Supplementary nutrition
Trout (smoked)
Walnuts
Walnuts roasted

11 Complementary

11.1 Aronia (Chokeberries)

Aronia arbutifolia und Aronia melanocarpa
Preparation: Instant drink
Against free radicals. Due to the high flavonoid, folic acid, vitamin K and vitamin C content, the Aronia is a medicinal plant. The
Aronia are available in the trade as dried berries, as juice concentrate, as tea and as a beverage.
Dosage: 1-2 glasses a day
Due to the high flavonoid, folic acid, vitamin K and vitamin C content, the Aronia is a medicinal plant. The Aronia are available in the trade as dried berries, as juice concentrate, as tea and as a beverage.

11.2 Bitter apricot seeds

Armeniacae Amarum, Semen
Preparation: Cooking addition
Relieves coughing and wheezing. Vitamin B17 against free radicals.
Dosage: 3-10 g (only after consultation with the doctor or therapist)
Notice: Do not overdose; not for children.

11.3 Candyleaf, sweetleaf, sugarleaf

Stevia rebaudiana
Preparation: Cooking addition
Sweetener for diabetics or for weight loss. Hypotensive, antimicrobial, vasodilator effect.
Attention - consult with your doctor or therapist.
Dosage: As sweetener, dried or fresh
Some studies have described teratogenic and mutagenic effects in hamsters and rats, as well as mutagenicity in vitro. Not authorized in the EU as food. Stevia supporters see behind it a conspiracy of sugar lobby and bias of the European Commission. Finally, stevioside has been used in Asia for decades as a sweetener - so far without negative consequences.
Notice: The WHO studies on the effects of steviol in vivo have not shown any evidence of mutagenic effects in humans. Only at your own risk.

11.4 Cannabis

Cannabis
Preparation: Healing tea (infusion)
High efficiency in combating chemotherapy-related side effects.
Analgesic.
Dosage: An incomprehensibly still controversial topic is the use of comparatively mild-acting marijuana in cancer, especially when one considers the consequences and scope of the everyday clinical use of morphine, a heroin-related substance. Marijuana showed directly tumor-inhibiting and life-prolonging effects in animal experiments. In addition, the drug contained in cannabis delta-9-tetrahydrocannbinol (THC) apparently suppresses the reproduction of gamma herpesviruses, which are suspected of causing cancer. The main use of cannabis in cancer, however, is its high efficiency in combating chemotherapy-related side effects. In the past, a number of medications - usually phenothiazines and butyrophenones - have been developed which should more or less successfully suppress these side effects, usually nausea and vomiting, however, according to scientists, the effect of cannabis seems to be clearly superior to these substances However, sometimes it requires dosages that make it possible to influence the central nervous system, ie it can come to a slight intoxication. In a randomized,
 double-blind study, 23 children in chemotherapy were given the synthetic cannabinoid 'nabilone' as an antidote to their chemotherapy-related side effects. 18 of them completed the study successfully. They all suffered from less nausea and vomiting than the children of the control group. Nabilone was also superior to comparable agents in 2/3 of them. Adverse effects were drowsiness and drowsiness.
Notice: It can come to a slight intoxication. The absorption of other medicines taken at the same time may be slowed or hindered. in case of overdose: nausea, vomiting, diarrhea, irritability.

11.5 Rooibos

Aspalathus linearis
Preparation: Healing tea (infusion)
Antioxidant, anti-inflammatory, anti-cancer, protects against flavanoids, also has a positive effect on Alzheimer's, arteriosclerosis. Antiallergic, inhibits histamine release. Antibacterial, antiviral, antifungal, detoxifying (alkaline).
Dosage: Brew 3-4 teaspoons of rooibos with one liter of boiling water and leave for 6-10 minutes. With soft water you need less tea for the preparation, with harder water we recommend a higher dosage.

12 Basics of Nutrition

The basic principles of nutrition described herein are general recommendations. They are not aimed at a specific form of therapy. Recommendations concerning a therapy have priority.

12.1 Nutrition

Regular meals in a relaxed atmosphere. A warm breakfast is considered a good start into the day.
The main meals ought to be taken for lunch – supper in the early evening. Pay attention to feeling hungry or sated: don't eat too much nor remain hungry is the rule
Prepare the meals freshly from natural, regional products. Frozen, heat-conserved, industrially prepared or foodstuffs cooked in the microwave oven are rejected.
Choice of foodstuffs according to the season: more cooling food in summer, more warming food in winter.
Eat cooked food at least twice a day. Food and drinks ought to be lukewarm, never ice-cold or hot.
Raw vegetables, briefly cooked vegetables, freshly squeezed juices and mineral water are not recommended. Milk and dairy products are only included in the diet if they don't cause problems.
Don't use therapeutic recipes over a longer period without consulting your doctor or therapist.

Varied food
Enjoy the diversity of foodstuffs. Characteristics of a balanced nutrition are variety, suitable combination and a balanced quantity of rich and low energy foodstuffs (on one hand avoiding undersupply with essential nutrients and on the other hand to take to many undesirable substances).

A lot of Cereal Products - and Potatoes
Bread, pasta, rice, cereal flakes (best wholemeal) as well as potatoes contain almost no fat, but many vitamins, mineral nutrients, trace elements, roughage and secondary plant substances. These foodstuffs ought to be taken with low-fat side dishes.

Vegetables and Fruit – „Take Five" every day ...
5 portions of vegetables and fruit a day, as fresh as possible, briefly cooked, or maybe one portion as a juice – ideal as a side dish to every meal as well as snack between meals: Thus a lot of vitamins, mineral nutrients as well as roughage and secondary plant substances

Daily milk and dairy products
Milk and Dairy Products every Day, once or twice per Week Fish; meat, sausages as well as eggs moderately. These foodstuffs contain valuable nutrients like calcium in the milk, iodine selenium and omega-3 fat acids in saltwater fish. Meat is favorable due to its high content of disposable iron and the vitamins B1, B6 and B12. Quantities of 300 – 600 g meat and sausage per week are sufficient. Prefer low-fat products, especially in meat- and dairy products.

Low-fat and fatty Foodstuffs
Fat supplies us with essential fat acids and fatty foodstuffs contain also fat-soluble vitamins. Fat is high in energy; therefore much fat in the food may cause overweight, possibly also cancer. Too many saturated fat acids may further a tendency for cardio-vascular diseases in the long term. Prefer vegetable oils and fats (e.g. rapeseed-, olive-, soya-oils and solid fats produced therefrom). Beware of invisible fat in meat- and dairy products, pastry and sweets as well as in fast-food and convenience foods. 70 – 90 g fat per day is sufficient.

Moderately Sugar and Salt
Take sugar and foods/drinks containing various kinds of sugar (e.g. glucose syrup) only occasionally. Use herbs and spices as well as a little salt creatively. Prefer salt containing iodine.

Plenty of Liquids
Water is absolutely essential. Drink 1-2 l liquids every day. Prefer water (with or without gas) and other low-calorie drinks. Alcoholic drinks should not be taken.

Tasty Dishes, carefully cooked
Cook the meals with as low temperatures and as short as possible, using little water and fat – this preserves the original taste, keeps the nutrients intact and prevents the production of harmful compounds.

Take time and enjoy the food
Take your Time and enjoy your Food
Eating consciously helps to eat right. The eye enjoys food, too. It's fun, invites to enjoy varied dishes and stimulates the feeling of satiety.

Watch your Weight and stay in Motion
A balanced diet and a lot of exercise and sport (30 – 60 min/day) are a healthy combination. The right weight furthers well-being and health. Thermals, directional effectiveness, digestive power

There are various criteria for judging the effectiveness of herbs and foodstuffs.
The use of certain herbs and ingredients is based on observations of the effects on the body which these foodstuffs, herbs and spices show after having eaten them. The medical science has developed following system: Every ingredient or herb has a directional effectiveness. Furthermore, there are herbs which have a special effect on certain organs.
The basic condition for a healthy metabolism is to obtain sufficient energy from food and that the digestive process doesn't use too much energy. An easily digestible meal makes content and sated, doesn't cause flatulence and fatigue after the meal. The perfect spices increase the healthiness of our meals. Very often, just small doses of herbs and spices will suffice. They are not used to make us sated, but to help our digestive organs to digest the food.

12.2 Recipes

The recipes list the ingredients to be used and the cooking instructions show how the dish is prepared. The list of ingredients shows the concerned quantities as well as the relevance for the therapy. If you find „less than mentioned", try to comply or find an alternative from the „list of recommended foodstuffs". Mostly it shall result just in a small change of taste when you simply avoid this ingredient.
Mild cooking methods: boiling, stewing, poaching, steaming
Strong cooking methods: barbecuing, roasting, frying, smoking
Balanced cooking methods: deep-frying, baking brick
Deep-freezing and warming in the microwave oven should be avoided (denaturalization).

12.3 Foodstuffs

Foodstuffs have an effect on body and soul like medicinal herbs, only a very much milder one. Dietary advice is mainly based on regional foodstuffs. The knowledge about the effects of each foodstuff and the knowledge, when which foodstuff shall be used, is based on the orthodoschool of medicine. Use ecologic-organic products, if possible. As everything should be cooked for a long time due to a better digestability and very rarely eaten raw, the food agrees with everyone.
The classification of the foodstuffs according to their effect on the body is the basis in order to achieve a harmonious status of health.

Dietary advisors do not recommend certain foodstuffs for everyone. The individual diet is tailor-made for the individual constitution.

Buy only fresh and ripe fruit and vegetables. You ought to leave unripe fruit and vegetables and such with brown spots and wilted leaves behind in the market. In this case take deep-frozen goods (never ready-to-serve dishes!). Fruit and vegetables are deep-frozen immediately after harvesting and often contain more vitamins and minerals than the goods from the vegetable shelf. Whereas conserved or tinned goods contain very much less biological substances. Also, salt, sugar and others are mostly added to the latter. Never leave the foodstuffs in the water after washing them to avoid that many vital substances get drowned. Clean salads, fruit and vegetables immediately before serving.

Please make sure of the hygienic processing of foodstuffs. Clean your salads, fruit and vegetables carefully. When cooking with meat, prepare all ingredients first and then process the meat products. Clean the worktop and tools very carefully. Wooden surfaces ought to be treated with a mild disinfectant regularly in order to reduce germination.

Store fruit and vegetables separately, if possible. Harvested fruit and vegetables are still alive and emit e.g. ethylene gas, which makes other products ripen and age faster. Keep meat and fish in the closed packaging or store them in the fridge in closed containers.

12.4 Herbs

There are some basic rules for storing medicinal herbs. On principle, herbs must be protected from direct sunlight, humidity and heat.

Containers for the storage of herbs may be glasses, ceramic jars and even plastic containers. However, plastic is a rather unsuitable material and should only be a short-term solution. In case of glass containers, use a dark material.

Medicinal herbs cannot be kept for any long period. The shelf life of herbs is limited. However, it can be prolonged with suitable storage. The place should be dark, rather cool and absolutely dry. A wooden medicine cabinet, placed not directly next to a source of heat, would be ideal. Never buy large quantities of herbs so as not to have to throw them away. Label the container with the name of the herb and the date of harvesting or processing.

13 Other dietic-books

The following syndromes of dietetics, TCM or for a therapy supplement for cancer are available.

Dietetics

E001. Nutrition of the infant - baby food
E002. Nutrition during lactation
E003. Nutrition in old age
E004. Nutrition of children and adolescents
E005. Nutrition of athletes
E006. Light weight
E007. Pregnancy
E008. Full food

Protein and electrolyte - kidneys
E009. (hemodialysis) dialysis treatment
E010. Acute renal failure
E011. Chronic renal insufficiency
E012. Nephrotic syndrome
E013. Kidney stones (nephrolithiasis)

Gastrointestinal tract - pancreas
E014. Acute pancreatitis (inflammation of the pancreas)
E015. Chronic pancreatitis (inflammation of the pancreas)

Gastrointestinal tract - small intestine and large intestine
E016. Acute obstipation (constipation)
E017. Chronic obstipation (constipation)
E018. Colon irritabile
E019. Diverticulitis
E020. Acquired lactose intolerance (lactose malabsorption)
E021. Fructose malabsorption
E022. Glutensensitive enteropathy (celiac disease)
E023. Colectomy
E024. Short Bowel Syndrome

Gastrointestinal tract - liver, gallbladder, bile ducts
E025. Acute and chronic hepatitis (inflammation of the liver)
E026. Cholelithiasis (bile stones)
E027. fatty liver
E028. cirrhosis

Gastrointestinal tract - Stomach and duodenal intestine
E029. Acute gastritis
E030. Chronic gastritis
E031. Stomach bleeding
E032. Ulcus ventriculi and duodenal ulcer
E033. Condition after gastric surgery

Gastrointestinal tract - oral cavity and esophagus
E034. Stomatitis
E035. Esophageal carcinoma (esophageal cancer)
E036. Refluosophagitis (heartburn)

Special diseases
E037. Phenylketonuria (PKU)
E038. Rheumatic joint diseases

Metabolism
E039. Obesity (overweight)
E040. Diabetes mellitus
E041. Eating disorders (underweight)

Fat metabolism
E042. Hypercholesterolaemia (increased cholesterol level)
E043. Hepatic Encephalopathy

Heart and circulation
E044. Arteriosclerosis (arterial calcification)
E045. Heart insufficiency
E046. Hypertension
E047. Hyperuricaemia and gout

Changed nutrient requirements
E048. In case of fever
E049. For malignant diseases
E050. After burns
E051. Radiation and chemotherapy

CANCER
E100. Pancreatic cancer
E101. Bladder cancer
E102. Blood cancer (leukemia)
E103. Breast cancer
E104. Colorectal cancer
E105. Gastric cancer
E106. Kidney cancer
E107. Esophageal cancer

TCM
E200. Bladder - moisture heat in the bladder
E201. Bladder - moisture and cold in the bladder
E202. Bladder - emptiness and cold in the bladder
E203. Large intestine - external cold affects the large intestine
E204. Large intestine - moisture heat in the large intestine
E205. Large intestine - heat blocks the intestine II acute
E206. Large intestine - dryness of the colon
E207. Large intestine - Yang deficiency (cold)
E208. Heart - Blood insufficiency
E209. Heart - Blood stagnation
E210. Heart - Fire
E211. Heart - Hot mucus clogs the heart pores

E212. Heart - Cold mucus clogs the heart pores
E213. Heart - Qi deficiency
E214. Heart - Yang deficiency
E215. Heart - Yin deficiency
E216. Liver - Ascending Liver Yang
E217. Liver - Blood deficiency
E218. Liver - Blood stagnation
E219. Liver - Moisture heat in liver and gall bladder
E220. Liver - Fire
E221. Liver - Gall bladder Qi-Empty
E222. Liver - Cold in the liver meridian
E223. Liver - Qi stagnation
E224. Liver - Wind
E225. Liver - Wind with ascending liver Yang
E226. Liver - Wind with blood anemic
E227. Liver - Wind with extreme heat
E228. Lung - Qi deficiency
E229. Lung - Mucus-moisture in the lungs
E230. Lung - Mucus-heat in the lungs
E231. Lung - Mucus-cold in the lungs
E232. Lung - Dryness of the lungs
E233. Lung - Wind-heat attacks the lungs
E234. Lung - Wind-cold affects the lungs
E235. Lung - Yin deficiency
E236. Stomach - Bloodstagnation
E237. Stomach - Fire
E238. Stomach - Cold with liquid
E239. Stomach - Nutrition stagnation
E240. Stomach - Qi deficiency
E241. Stomach - Rebellious Qi
E242. Stomach - Yin Emptiness
E243. Spleen - Heat and moisture attack the spleen
E244. Spleen - Coldness and moisture affects the spleen
E245. Spleen - Qi deficiency
E246. Spleen - Qi deficiency + Declining spleen Qi
E247. Spleen - Qi deficiency + spleen does not control the blood
E248. Spleen - Yang deficiency
E249. Kidney - Heart and kidney no longer communicate
E250. Kidney - Jing deficiency
E251. Kidney - Kidneys cannot receive the Qi
E252. Kidney - Qi is not stable
E253. Kidney - Yang deficiency
E254. Kidney - Yin deficiency

For further information visit di-book.com.

14 EBNS - Software for nutritional counseling

The main task of the database is to create personalized nutritional advice for each patient individually. The database was developed for Dietetics and Traditional Chinese Medicine.

The Database supports training and advices in the daily work routine.

The computer program provides lists of recipes, ingredients and herbs, which are given to the client. individually adjustable according to patient's request from whole food to vegetarians (lacto, ovo, ...). For every register there is an information sheet which can be given to the client. All texts can be individually designed.

The syndromes can be combined and result in an intersection of the recommended recipes and ingredients. The automated diagnosis for the TCM enables you to check your experience during the training as well as to confirm your diagnosis in the working day. You select several predefined symptoms and have the program automatically display the relevant syndromes.

How to work with the database:
Select the patient / client, select one or more of the syndromes you diagnosed and print the folder.

You can change all values, create new symptoms or syndromes, develop recipes, change or adapt ingredients and herbs to your findings. In simple client management, all relevant data about the person is stored. You get an overview of the past diagnoses and the development of the course of the disease.

As a consultant you save a lot of time when you print out the recipe, food and herbal lists for the recognized syndromes and give them to the clients. You can use this time for a personal conversation. With the database, dieticians and nutritionists can view the nutrients and trace elements for each recipe and develop recipes for syndromes even with suggested ingredients.

All recipe and grocery lists can also be ordered from me as a combination of several diseases. I wish all readers good luck, health and happiness in life.
More information can be found at www.ebns.at.
Volunteer: www.krebsinfo.at
Josef Miligui